Ghosts in the 'Ville

True Experiences of the Unexplained in Riegelsville, Pennsylvania

Jeffrey A. Wargo

Enjoy! Jeffry A Wargo

10/06

PublishAmerica
Baltimore

First printing

ISBN: 1-4137-4283-1
PUBLISHED BY PUBLISHAMERICA, LLLP
www.publishamerica.com
Baltimore

Printed in the United States of America

For Stephanie Anne, my wonderful wife,
soul mate, and partner, whose love was so great
as to marry me and move into a haunted house…

Ghosts in the 'Ville is intended for entertainment purposes only. All accounts contained herein are accurate to the best of the recollections of this author and those involved. They have been obtained through personal interviews and the sharing of stories.

Special Thanks to Stephanie Anne, for her encouragement, love, and support.

Special Thanks to Mom and Dad, Dave and Katie, Curt, Sara, Debbie Jo, Ann Louise, Ann, Craig, Greg, the good folk at St. John UCC and the Riegelsville Public Library, and all those who have shared their ghostly tales! Continue to learn more about the ghosts in Riegelsville and share your stories! This book would not be possible without you.

Special Thanks also to Stephanie Burke, owner of Lasting M 'Pressions Photography, who provided the author's picture for the book cover and publicity

The Historical Information in this text is gathered from materials shared in the Riegelsville Public Library's House Tour booklets from 1986 and 1992, and from the church record at St. John United Church of Christ. Other historical information is gathered from several books of the town's history, buildings, and people. I have documented each book as it has been used in the text.

The old town photos throughout the text are loaned from the private collection of Riegelsville resident Ann Anderson and are used with permission.

www.ghostsintheville.com

Table of Contents

Preface 9

Foreword 11

Terror in the Night.. 15

A History Retold. 22

First Encounters 30

Rocking in the Gray Morn 36

Cool Breeze on My Shoulder 38

A Ghostly Commentary 41

Men's Voices 46

A Face in the Window 49

Footsteps Yet Again. 50

Henry's Nose... 52

The Evil One 54

Married Haunting 57

Hearing the Stories 60

The Figure in Black 64

The Uninvited Guest 67

The Church Ghost 70

Alarming Office Behavior 77

Opening Doors 86

Ghost Tours and Detection 90

A Treasury of Tales 95

The John S. Riegel Estate... 102

The Riegelsville Academy Building 109

Restoration Ruminations 115

The Riegelsville Inn 118

The Riegelsville Fire Company.. 123

The Old Kohl Bakery 126

The Riegel Building 129

The Union Cemetery 131

Stories Told, Retold, and Untold. 135

Preface

Ghost stories, or stories about the supernatural, often create a sense of fear in individuals who hear about or read them. This book, a collection of stories, is not meant to scare you. It is simply a recording of experiences as individuals encountered them. Are they true? They are true in the sense that every individual has a perceived reality. The experiences that we have determine what is "true" for us.

For the individuals who have shared their tales in this text, their experiences were real and hence, true. Many of the tales come from public buildings where a great many people live, work, and move about each day and week without incident or an inkling of "spirits."

I wish to thank all of the many folk who have shared their stories with me over the years in good faith, good humor, and with a truly genuine nature. It is my hope that this folklore of Riegelsville will continue to live on, as apparently many of its spirits do.

But by all means, when you have learned of these tales, please respect the privacy of the individuals now living or working in these places. Many of them have experienced nothing out of the ordinary and would discount the tales of others. For them, these stories are but the imagination at work.

These stories are presented for you to read as single chapters that stand alone, or as one continuous tale. They are shared as entertainment and are not meant to defame, insult, or otherwise detract from the character or nature of the individuals, living or dead, in relation to the situations described. You may consider them pure fiction and pure imagination if you like.

But whether born of imagination and fancy or true by perception and experience, I share with you these tales of the unknown in Riegelsville.

Pull up a chair. Grab a blanket. Turn off all but one light. Enjoy!

Foreword

Ghosts. The very mention of them piques the curiosity of some people, frightens others, and is the subject of jokes and speculation for many more.

From the earliest time I can remember, I was intrigued by stories about ghosts and supernatural phenomena. As a young child, I would sit with my heart in my throat, wide-eyed, as the older kids I knew terrorized my friends and me with stories of ghosts in the homes around our town. I sat at the mirror for hours in the night waiting to see the ghostly apparition of "Bloody Mary" after chanting the ritual they prescribed, and I participated in the party game *Light as a Feather*, anxious to see a body lifted by several solitary fingers. As if that wasn't enough, my heart would often freeze as the older kids would rattle a garage door along one of the dark and secluded alleys in town and tell me that the sounds I heard next were bones rattling (today I know they were nails in a jar on a shelf inside the door).

Looking back, I know that all of these early exposures to the supernatural were nothing more than elaborate and well thought-out hoaxes aimed at scaring young children. I never dreamed that I would have firsthand experience with the real thing.

Yet even before I was old enough for words, I believe I had already been exposed to the true presence of the supernatural. This revelation came to me during a lunch visit with my brother, shortly before I sat down to write this book.

During our meal, he shocked me by asking if I had ever seen any ghosts in the home in which we grew up. I prompted him to tell me why he was asking such a question and his response was a story so chilling it made the hair stand up on the back of my neck.

He remembered an experience from childhood of waking up in the middle of the night to find a dark figure standing over him near his bed. He blinked several times and finally it disappeared. The thought of someone standing over you while you sleep is chilling enough as it is, but it was compounded for me because for a long time I had been tormented when I closed my eyes by images in my head of a dark silhouette standing over me. When the images would come, the feelings that accompanied them made me sure that I was lying in my crib at the time of the incidents. I asked my brother to describe where my crib was in the room without telling him my recollections. Once he did, I was further amazed to learn that the image in my head coincided exactly with the placement of my crib in our bedroom. The dark silhouette of my subconscious may actually have been a recollection of an experience from my early childhood. It's hard to tell, but eerie nonetheless.

As a young teenager, I listened with amazement to stories from my peers about their ghostly experiences through the medium of a Ouija board. Their tales of spectral visions, prankster ghosts, and innocent contacts scared me enough to give me a healthy respect for these things, such that a Ouija board is something I will never own or allow in my home. Yet I must admit that, despite my respect for the power of the unknown, these experiences did not prevent me from reading ghost stories for leisure and delighting in movies about the phenomena.

My first adult experience of the real thing though, came during my years at Princeton Theological Seminary.

A colleague was house-sitting for the summer in a town in central New Jersey. He had gone there early in June and was present very little on campus. But as the summer progressed, he seemed to spend more and more time on the seminary grounds. It became strange because sometimes late into the evening he would be found still on campus despite the hour. Then one day he announced that he was transferring schools. Some mutual friends decided they wanted to visit him to say goodbye before he left. They were invited to come to the house where he was staying, but were strongly cautioned that if he was not yet home, they were not to go inside the dwelling without him and were given strict parameters as to how long they could stay.

The visit they describe is hair-raising. Upon their arrival, two of my friends entered the home despite the host's absence. After looking around, they decided to check out the second floor and went to the staircase at the center of the house. There they described an energy pushing against them as they attempted to go up the steps. Our mutual friend was upset when he arrived and learned that they had ventured inside. Later, he spoke about needing to be careful about what he said and did because the spirits would take revenge on him if he stepped beyond the boundaries they had set.

After visiting for a time and sharing in dinner, the friends decided to pray with our colleague. In the midst of the prayer, a force seemed to be trying to push their circle apart. Prayer seemed to be forbidden by some unseen presence in the house. Even more chilling, it seemed that our colleague had taken to sleeping in the kitchen of this country home despite the fact that all his possessions were on the second floor. Further, he would not allow his guests into certain rooms because of "bad things" that had happened there. Our mutual friends experienced unexplainable shadows and oil lights that went on and off on their own.

As they left for the evening they said our friend walked them to the door, shutting off all the lights as they moved toward the outside. When my friends got into their car, their host turned to go back inside, and while he was yet in the driveway, they were startled to see the lights on the second floor turn themselves back on.

A day or two after this incident, I was taken to this home by one of our mutual friends who needed to revisit the site to show me firsthand how creepy it really seemed. It was late in the evening on a dry night when we ventured back the wooded lane to the home nestled in the trees. Under my friend's direction, I pulled up onto the driveway and was amazed when my car seemed to take on a life of its own. It couldn't be steered, but only skidded back and forth. Finally, after I managed to catch my breath and turn the car around and get back onto the empty road, I was startled by the sudden appearance of another car in my rearview window; it's headlights blinding me in the darkness. What's more, the car seemed to materialize out of nowhere. As we drove the quarter mile back to the highway, the phantom car suddenly disappeared again!

A year later, after our friend had transferred elsewhere, I chose to tell some first year seminarians about the experience we had endured at this country home. Their curiosity raised, we got in the car and ventured out to the property to look around. To our amazement it was for sale and after some smooth talking, we managed to get a tour from the homeowner.

As we moved through the first floor to the staircase at the heart of the house, I suddenly became sick to my stomach and was overcome with a feeling of melancholy. Yet after climbing the stairs the feeling ceased. The sickness only returned again on the journey back down the steps to the first floor and disappeared once I crossed the threshold to the room beyond. I cannot say what caused it, but a smothering feeling came along with it and it only happened in the stairwell area of the home. I believe there was a spiritual unrest in that particular part of the house and nothing will convince me otherwise.

I prayed I would never experience such a smothering feeling again.

In April 1996, I accepted a call as pastor to a small Delaware Valley borough in upper Bucks County, Pennsylvania. In July of that same year, I moved into town.

This book is a collection of the experiences that came to light in the years that followed. Some are ordinary, some extraordinary. They chronicle the unexplainable phenomena in the parsonage of St. John United Church of Christ and the other church properties. They also tell the stories of others in the community who have experienced the unexplainable.

In a borough of nine hundred, where over a thousand lay buried in the cemetery within its limits, the stories remind us that the dead outnumber the living and, in this community at least, that overpopulation means that some of those spirits still seek to live among us.

Terror in the Night

The Delaware Valley hides a treasure trove of scenic spots that can enthrall those who travel the busy Route 611 corridor south along the old Delaware Canal to the junction of Route 32 and on to historic Philadelphia. Many small towns dot the Delaware River banks in Pennsylvania and New Jersey, and each one contains its vault of stories from days gone by and lives enjoyed in their years.

Yet there is no place where the vault seems as full of untold tales as it does in the borough of Riegelsville. In this sleepy little paper mill town, many whisper stories about days gone by and of lives enjoyed in years past. Trouble is, many of those lives seem too restless to remain in the past, causing their spirits to roam about in that hazy realm between reality and the netherworld, much to the chagrin of many a building's residents.

One good example is the house that stands atop a slight hill in the borough, overlooking the historic Cook farm. The building seems to mold itself into what some call Mansion Row. Its two and one-half story fieldstone exterior, dotted with windows, and covered with old gabled slate roofs is eye catching to the passerby with its maroon shutters and white woodwork.

Erected in 1887 on the north end of a two acre lot of land donated by John L. Riegel to the St. John Reformed Church to house its pastors, this present day structure is an impressive eighteen room edifice (Cook, Kathleen. Riegelsville, PA: It's Buildings and Early Inhabitants. 1991: Riegelsville Academy Library Fund, page 134). Its twelve-foot high ceilings and hardwood floors feel the rattle of the trucks as they travel the highway on their journeys. Their creaks and groans may deceptively cause the building's residents to attribute strange noises to the nearby highway traffic or to settling. But those who have resided there, myself included, can tell of other sources… other things that go bump in the night.

Tuesday, July 16, 1996, was a day of celebration for me as I settled in to this immense home in my first days as the new parish pastor in town. My parents had stayed with me the previous weekend through all the glorious confusion of moving in but had since gone home to let me get settled, and I grew more excited and even more anxious to get unpacked and hang my hat after seven years of living in dormitories and waiting for a place to live that I could call my own. Little did I know that this would be a home that I would have to share with a housemate—one unseen and unexplainable.

After a night of teaching Vacation Bible School at the church building just slightly down the road, several members of the congregation who had been teaching sat with me around a table in the church's social room reflecting upon the day's activities. One of the women there inquired as to how I felt about visitors at the parsonage, because my predecessor had hosted many. I responded that I didn't mind visitors and, in fact, was excited to have some since the thought of meeting new people and making connections had appeal in a town where I knew very few. I didn't know the question had held a double entendre. If I did, it would have better prepared me for the terror about to come.

I arrived home sometime after 9 P.M. and began to sort through more boxes before, exhausted and sticky from the heat, I took a hot shower and retired to one of the upstairs bedrooms of the house for a much needed night's rest.

Admittedly a little on edge about being in a big house for the first night by myself, I left the door to my bedroom open. There were no expected phone calls to wake me, no alarm clock to get me up, no agenda for the following day. I planned to sleep late, unpack more, and enjoy the two weeks I had before my ministry officially began.

As I remember it, sleep came easy that night. The sounds of the traffic moving along outside the screened windows soon soothed me to a deep slumber and I drifted off into dreamland. My bed lay situated with the headboard against the hall wall of the bedroom, the open door to the hall on my right. I'm not sure how long I slept but then again, the events of the next few hours made the night seem like eternity.

I realized later that it was sometime around 1:30 A.M., when I became conscious of a rhythmic noise emanating from above me in the house. In that netherworld between being awake and asleep, my mind rolled around trying to identify the sound and focus on it. I was startled to realize that I was listening to the sound of ominous and reverberating footsteps on the hardwood floor in the vacant room above me! They sounded as if the person was walking back and forth above the length of my bed. I sat bolt upright.

Watching the clock, I was aware that the sound went on for almost two minutes while I sat stiff as a board, the sudden cold of the room causing the hair on my neck to stand on end. I listened for a time, my fear increasing as I had no way to defend myself and no phone to call for help. I pressed my back up against the hall wall and listened as the footsteps exited the room above me and moved to the top of the stairs heading down from the third floor. The deep echoes increased in volume as, one at a time, the stairs caught the footfalls of the intruder descending them. Not knowing what else to do, I began to pray in earnest, "Our Father, who art in heaven…"

My prayer was nearly reaching its end and the footfalls were growing closer to the bottom when all of a sudden it got deathly quiet again. I shivered under my covers, petrified as to who was in my home—my mind swirling with apprehension, my heart held fast in its place by a grip of death.

The night passed long as I drifted in and out of light sleep, constantly afraid to close my eyes and relax my safety vigil.

At the earliest rays of sunlight, I rose quickly and opened the attic door—nothing was there. Not wishing to explore any further, I quickly showered and dressed, then headed downstairs for breakfast. Nothing had been disturbed.

Finally my need for knowledge and explanation won out and I hurried over to the church and inquired to one of the people there,

Fig 1. Main St. In Riegelsville, PA (Courtesy of Ann Anderson).

"Did my predecessor ever speak of strange noises in the parsonage?"

The reply took my breath. "Oh you met the ghost?"

"It is a ghost?" I replied.

"Yes," they said.

"Your predecessor said there were two of them and one wasn't very nice."

I absorbed what I heard and I think blocked out any more information. Returning home, I called my seminary friends and bragged about the ghost in my home, trying to convince myself that this was cool. They reminded me that upon visiting the home at my interview, I shared with them that the place had felt haunted. I don't recall saying such a thing, but it is entirely possible.

The day passed rather quickly as I worked to finalize plans for ordination the following Sunday and continued unpacking the many boxes of personal items that still waited for a place in the home.

As the afternoon began to fade into the shadows of evening and I sat down to rest in what I had established as a sitting room on the first floor, a foreboding presence began to make itself known.

It was about 4 o'clock in the afternoon and the sun descending was

18

Fig 2. The Parsonage. Built in 1887 by St. John Reformed Church.

beginning to cast shadows through one second story hall window and down the staircase. As I rested in the sitting room, a cold clammy feeling seemed to permeate the space around me and the walls began to feel as if they were closing in.

The memory of that smothering feeling from the previous year's visit to that country home in New Jersey came rushing back, as a similar feeling settled in around me. The home took on a personality—almost a feeling of evil. If it were only my impressions, I would chalk them up to being alone in a home for the first time and to mental anguish over the night before. But I was excited about my new ministry, captivated by the home, and eager to make it mine. Yet this foreboding feeling shook me to my core.

Months later I learned that one minister who preceded my coming had visited the parsonage during its renovations and was overcome by the sensation that they were not welcome. In fact, the feeling was so strong that they had to leave. We shared this feeling. I packed a bag very quickly and left for the 65-mile journey to my parent's home.

That night was long, even in the familiar surroundings of my childhood space. Every time I closed my eyes, I could hear those footsteps on the wooden floors echoing in my mind and I could feel the cold.

The next day I called my predecessor and learned that he, too, had encountered strange happenings in the home. I wrestled with the question of whether or not I could, in fact, live in the house and be comfortable. Several phone calls later a colleague recommended that I see a psychologist. Reluctantly I went.

He challenged me to stay at the house one night and offered me the lifeline that if things got uncomfortable, I could call him. I went back to the house that afternoon. Pulling the car into the driveway, I had the sensation of being watched by some unseen presence looking out one of the upstairs windows. Yet I gathered my courage and went inside.

At first things seemed okay.

But as the sun set and the shadows descended down the long stairwell at the center of the house, that cold foreboding feeling returned. I quickly decided that it wasn't a good idea to stay and called the psychologist, telling him that the deal was off. Again I left, feeling that I would have to resign my position and move and wondering how I was ever going to get my things out of the house without staying there.

That evening I shared dinner with my parents once again and tried to assure them that I wasn't crazy but couldn't live with this situation. After some time of reflection, in what might have seemed a headstrong moment, I determined I would return and claim the space as my own. Without giving myself time to change my mind, I drove quickly back to Riegelsville with the intention to stay the night.

I guess my brother was worried for my safety and, I am sure, just a bit curious about my story. He called my predecessor who lived only a short distance from the parsonage and asked him to meet us there. Then he followed me back to Riegelsville.

I arrived back at the house just as it was growing dark and gathered my courage once again. Then I went inside. In a short time my brother and predecessor arrived. My predecessor then shared with me some of the strange experiences he had during his residency in the parsonage. He encouraged me not to be scared and offered the assurance that he had never been harmed.

Soon I began to feel more comfortable and he left for the night. I retired to a different bedroom in the back of the house that night—a room I would occupy for the next six months. My brother slept in the

20

front room where my terror of two nights past had occurred. A late evening rain set in and began pounding on the slate roof outside the second floor windows, its rhythm gently soothing me to sleep. A peaceful night passed.

The next morning I awoke refreshed and a little more courageous. Going down the hall to the room where I had encountered the strange sounds, I found my brother wide-awake and rattled. He hadn't heard anything or seen anything unusual, but he hadn't slept either—and he even had his pet beagle with him in the room! Later that day he left for home. I went to a local bookstore and purchased a book on spiritual warfare and house blessing.

Now it may seem a bit strange, but in talking with the local priest in town and one in nearby Easton, I learned that it would be best if I blessed the house myself, thereby claiming my space.

Returning home, I took a bottle of holy water from my recent journey to the Jordan River and, using those spiritual prayers in the book I had purchased, I began the long climb to the third floor to begin the ritual.

The summer heat was intense on the third floor in all except the room where the noises had been heard. That room felt cold and clammy when I entered. Beginning there and summoning my strength, I invoked God's presence and began the ritual—sprinkling holy water, saying the prayers, and marking each doorframe with the sign of the cross in a circle. In a short time I had blessed the entire house from the room in the attic where the noises had been, to the threshold of the front door—every room, every closet, every hallway.

Stepping out of the house into the summer sun, it felt as if a warm presence wrapped itself around me. Turning, I re-entered the house. The overwhelming evil presence that had felt so smothering was gone. In fact I have not felt it since that day. Yet there was still the feeling of being watched in the house. I know for sure that the spirit intent on not sharing the home is gone. It felt good to know that it would not be back. But there was another....

A History Retold

It is well documented in many books and by paranormal investigators that times of remodeling or returning land to its original condition can arouse supernatural and spiritual incidents in a place or home. During these periods, psychic activity seems to increase and visions, sounds, and happenings seem to occur with more frequency.

In the three years between my predecessor's retirement and my arrival, the church completed a project of remodeling parts of the parsonage and repairing other sections of the structure. Fresh paint was applied to all the walls and woodwork. The kitchen was remodeled and a door removed. The bathroom was touched up and repaired; the second floor was painted; the carpeting was replaced; and the hallway floors were polished. The third floor was left alone. It seems only fitting then that the spirits would come to explore, to enchant, or perhaps even to scare those working in their beloved space.

During the time of renovations, church folk spent many long hours in the parsonage. Sometimes they worked alone and sometimes they worked in teams. Many say they experienced nothing out of the ordinary during their times in the house. Yet from that renovation period, two stories have emerged which at the time still did not seem to convince the church's members that something strange was really going on within the walls of this home, even though my predecessor had shared his experiences with congregation members, friends, and others in the community. I believe they thought he was joking.

However the joke must not have been very funny to an unfortunate member of the renovation team who was working alone in an upstairs bedroom of the house. He describes painting in the room, only to sense a presence right behind him. Turning, he saw nothing there. He tried again to work, and still the annoying feeling of someone nearby troubled him. He took a break and went downstairs to rest. A short time later he returned to the room. But after only a few moments, it seemed that the presence had returned and was watching him yet again. The previous pastor returned for some personal items around this time and while he was in the house, this worker commented about the strange feelings he had been experiencing, only then learning about the ghost. He never returned to work again.

His task was picked up by an older gentleman whose hard work was frustrated by the fact that, every time he'd climb a ladder to paint the bedroom door, the door would pop open on him. He tried to close that door many times and keep it closed so that his job could be finished, but it just seemed that someone or something wanted the door open. He eventually propped the door closed by placing the ladder in front of it, thus completing the job.

And while the psychic activity in the parsonage seemed to increase during the renovation period, there is eyewitness testimony to the fact that the spirits were active in the house well *before* the period of remodeling. Consider some of the tales my predecessor told us the night he sat with my brother and me, trying to convince me I had nothing to fear.

My predecessor moved to the church parsonage with his family in the early 1960s and took up residence. He shared with me that many a night as he lay sleeping, he would hear those familiar footsteps echo through the house as some unseen guest traveled on its late night walk from the third floor. It would move slowly through the second floor halls and pass family members' beds, before descending to the first floor and disappearing. Many a night he grabbed a bat and went looking to nab the intruder only to find empty rooms and nothing disturbed. His wife also commented on the presence she felt in the house and together they regarded it with some curiosity.

One night, to his surprise, as he awoke and ventured out onto the second floor landing to explore the strange noises, he looked down the stairs and saw a woman dressed in what can be described as black mourning clothes, complete with a shawl, looking up at him. He called out to her and she then turned and moved into the living room below. When he ran down the stairs to see if she was there, the figure was gone!

Two of his three children have also shared tales with us as they visited my wife and me over the last seven years. One son recalls a time when he was younger and encountered the house's ghost. It was late in the evening as he stood at the top of the staircase in the second floor bathroom, brushing his teeth and getting ready for bed. Looking up into the wall sized bathroom mirror, he was startled to see in its reflection, a misty apparition standing on the opposite end of the hall outside his bedroom door. The figure appeared to be a woman, wearing a Victorian style dress with a hoop skirt. She stood at the end of the hallway near the door to the third floor staircase. He said she looked peaceful, but frightened him. The apparition went into a room and vanished.

The other son confirmed hearing the noises of footsteps coming down the third floor stairs and stopping just inside the doorway.

One day he asked his dad, "Why do you go to the third floor after we go to sleep, and how come you never open the door when you come back down?"

To his surprise, his dad told him he hadn't been on the third floor at all!

Guests of the family also were not immune to the ghostly sightings. One woman, who was staying with my predecessor and his family for a visit and sleeping in a bedroom on the third floor, was troubled throughout the night by what she thought was the sound of someone in the family shifting items around in the other rooms near her.

The next morning, she came to breakfast and asked my predecessor, "Why were you moving furniture outside my room last night?"

"I was doing nothing of the sort," came the shocking response.

"That must have been Louisa." This was the name my predecessor had given to the phantom he had seen at the bottom of the stairs.

The houseguest allegedly said she would never stay on the third floor again.

It's strange, but the third floor of the parsonage really does seem to have more peculiar and unexplainable activity than other parts of the house. My predecessor relates that, as he was starting to prepare to move his residency from the home, he had put some furniture up on that very floor. The furniture could later be heard moving around while no living person was up there. What's more is that things seemed to be moved out of place or thrown around when he eventually did go back up there.

Another tale shared is that of a day when one of the pastor's children had friends over to play in the first floor room I was currently using as a sitting room. At that time the room had been decorated with plush blue carpet and antiques, and the portrait of a woman hung on one of the walls. The pastor's son had gotten up and gone to the kitchen for a drink, leaving his friends alone in the room. While he was there, he was surprised when all of his friends ran from the house, terrified and screaming. They later told him that, when he had left them alone, the room grew cold and footsteps began to appear in the blue shag rug as if someone was walking toward the portrait.

Thus, after a night of storytelling, I came to learn that I shared this elegant house with a woman who had apparently been given the name Louisa. My predecessor claimed that she was buried behind St. John church in the oldest part of the union cemetery and told me where to find her grave. Louisa seemed to be the most logical choice for the presence because, in the church history, she was the only woman he could find who had died in her home while living on one of the church properties. It was not long before I began to grow curious and seek the story of this mysterious ghostly figure. An interesting history then unfolded before me.

It seems that "Louisa" was possibly Mary Louisa Aughinbaugh, the sister of the Rev. Dr. E.E. Higbee (Fackenthal, B.F., Jr. Saint John Reformed Church of Riegelsville, PA. 1911: Eschenbach Printing Co:

25

Easton, PA. Page 118.) and the wife of the Rev. George W. Aughinbaugh, who was called to St. John as pastor in January 1862, while the church was yet a union parish of Lutheran and Reformed members (Osborn, Arthur. Riegelsville: People, Places and Events. 1960: Democrate Press: Flemington, NJ, Page 29).

Mary Louisa and George were the first pastoral couple to occupy the Cyrus S. Stover house when St. John Reformed Church purchased the building for its use as a parsonage. Cyrus Stover's widow sold it to the church in 1864. (Cook 137, Fackenthal 43–44).

As the church records indicate, Rev. Aughinbaugh was very much involved in civil affairs and education. He was a strong Union man who had come north from his home in the Shenandoah Valley after the Civil War broke out in 1861. Born in 1819, he graduated from Marshall College in 1844, and from the Theological Seminary at Lancaster in 1846 (Fackenthal 44). After the battle of Antietam, the people of Riegelsville sent him to Maryland to look after their own among the sick and wounded from Company C, 128th Regiment, Pennsylvania Volunteers (Fackenthal 46).

Little is written about Mary Louisa except that, after Rev. Aughinbaugh resigned in 1864 to accept the presidency of the Heidelburg College in Tiffin, Ohio, the records indicate that she found the climate of their new home area detrimental to her health (Osborn 31). The story goes that Mary Louisa loved Riegelsville very much and wanted it to be her home forever. The climate was right and the town was to her liking.

On November 5, 1865, Rev. Aughinbaugh wrote to the church to see if there was any chance of his returning to St. John as pastor, and he was called back to Riegelsville to resume his ministry (Osborn 31, Fackenthal 47). In the months that followed, he and Mary Louisa shared the joy of parenthood with at least two children, Charles and Martha (Fackenthal 119), and then tragedy struck. Mary Louisa succumbed to tuberculosis on September 19, 1867, at the age of 41. She was buried in the Riegelsville Cemetery (Fackenthal 47).

The church record goes on to share that George Auginbaugh grieved over the loss of his beloved wife. He was married again, however, in 1872, to a woman named Emma Keely. She joined the church in November of that year and, before the following year had passed, the Rev. and new Mrs. Aughinbaugh moved away after he accepted yet another collegiate presidency at Palatinate College in 1873 (Fackenthal 55–56, 197).

But the Aughinbaugh's ministry with the congregation of St. John church never really ended. It seems that Mary Louisa began an eternal ministry of looking after her husband and his new family in this little Delaware River town. Upon his departure, it is said that her spirit remained to keep watch over those who would live and work in the house and church that she loved.

The woman in dark clothing that the previous pastor encountered is indeed perhaps the spirit of Mary Louisa, who seeks to be a caretaking presence for the pastors of the church and their families, as she eternally wanders around the church grounds.

Some would say the spirit is more deliberate in its path, and not so much wandering. It is reported that the ghost of a woman has been spotted walking on a route between the buildings of the church properties and the corner of the Union Cemetery. There, a conspicuous headstone designates Mary Louisa's final resting place.

The marker is unique. It is composed of white fieldstone boulders, roughly piled together into a cube. A shield is askew on the front of the boulders and upon it is written her date of death. Above the boulders, a flower is carved into the stone. The edifice is topped with a rough stone cross that is designed to resemble a tree wrapped in vines.

One recent visitor to her burial place shared that his first impressions upon seeing the marker were feelings of anger. He described the faux wooden cross and vines, which sit atop the boulders, as a traditional symbol of the Victorian period, representing the fact that the person buried in that grave, had died young. He also observed that the stone seems to have been "thrown together" and have a fluid motion.

The church record states that the membership of St. John erected the tombstone and financed its construction because of their affection for Mary Louisa.

Fig 3. Gravestone of Mary Louisa Aughinbaugh, Union Cemetery, Riegelsville, PA.

The inscription reads:

In Glory.
Mary Louisa,
wife of Rev. G. W. Aughinbaugh,
Pastor of Reformed Church.
Died September 19, 1867.
I believe in the communion of saints.

Her husband George lies beside her with his own headstone marker. The inscription on his marker reads:

Rev. G. W. Aughinbaugh, DD.
Feb 12, 1819 to August 28, 1913
Pastor of
St. John Reformed Church, Riegelsville, PA
January 1862 to July 1865
November 1865 to April 1873

It is curious to note that Mary Louisa's gravestone does not indicate her date of birth, or reflect any indication of her life other than that she was a pastor's wife and that she died. I believe that for her, the grave is not a comfortable place of rest because her final marker shows nothing to reflect her vitality and her love of life.

Perhaps she still wanders about so that people remember that she lived. Perhaps she wanders about in the eternal, dedicated role of pastor's wife, indeed seeking to watch over and care for those who live in the congregation that she served. Perhaps she's looking for George.

The history leads one to wonder....

First Encounters

My early feeling regarding the spirits with whom I shared my home was one of curiosity coupled with sheer terror. In the first months I lived in the parsonage, its pale walls would take on an ominous grayish tone in the shadowy hours of dusk. By nightfall, I had on every light in the house, and didn't venture into rooms that were dark without the benefit of a light switch right inside the door. But even turning on a light did little to illumine the darkness I experienced in my mind whenever night would fall. It was as if the home had two personalities: its daytime persona and its nighttime one. The daily persona was one of history, beauty, and comfort. The nightly one was one of uncertainty, tension so thick it was palpable, and extreme discomfort. The spirits communicated well that I was a stranger in their home. I always felt watched and never knew what was coming next. The tension affected my sleep, and I am sure, my psyche.

Perhaps the most disturbing piece of this whole new living orientation for me was my perception that some members of the congregation, even though they had heard stories from the previous pastor, seemed to think I was joking about the ghost. It must have seemed strange to them to have a young professional so disturbed with a house as to consider leaving a new job, but it was even stranger to me that they didn't seem to truly believe that the spirits were even here.

In order to help me adjust to these new living conditions, and perhaps out of fear that the new pastor would quickly leave, one kind person in the church recommended I adopt a cat.

After another night of sleeping with all the house lights on, the clock radio playing loudly, and the door closed (anxiety brewing every time I had to leave the room), the need for sanity won out, and I adopted a kitten. I can't say getting a kitten was the most logical answer to my situation, for I truly believed an exorcism or spiritual intervention would have made more sense, but it was a far easier endeavor than seeking an exorcist who could potentially disturb the spirits more and cause greater duress under which I would have to live. So far the spirits hadn't hurt me, and with my healthy respect for the power and stories of ghosts I had heard of in years past, I decided not to go that route. At least now there was another living creature in the house that could create noise, provide me a logical explanation for sounds, and create an endless supply of laughter and enjoyment.

It wasn't long before one cat grew to three and soon I felt more comfortable because there was so much life present in the cavernous space I called home.

I gave each of the cats a jingle bell on its collar so that when I heard thumping in the halls at night, I could tell if it was my family or something unseen roaming about. I also named them in a tongue and cheek manner, as they were there to alleviate my fears when day turned to night. I called them Evening, Nightshade, and Snuggle--perfect names for cats whose purpose was to comfort and protect their master in the dark hours of slumber. The cats adjusted well and helped me to adjust better also. In time, I was turning off the lights to go to bed and even leaving my door slightly ajar so that the cats could come and go as they pleased.

Before many months had passed, I finally settled in to a regular life as the new parish minister in town. It became apparent to me that the ghosts were not there to frighten or alarm me. Rather it seemed that we were cohabitating in the same building, but in truly different periods or realms of time. It also became apparent that, unlike the stories I had read about hauntings that occur over specific intervals and on certain days or hours, the ghost in this house could never really be counted on to do anything. In some ways, that made living with it easier because it took away the anticipation of night after night encounters.

Yet there was one small exception to the lack of patterned supernatural activity. For the first three weeks I lived in the home, every evening I would return from the church or a walk to find all of the basement lights on, each of which had an independent switch! I would see them glowing along the foundation of the parsonage as I approached. They were like yellow eyes peering through the dusk of the evening watching for me to welcome me home. It was almost as if the spirits were saying they missed me. I would have to go down every night and shut each light off, before settling in to bed and trying to get some sleep.

After a short period, the evening light-show ended. Yet the attraction to lights never really did stop. I remember once, in early August, on a Saturday afternoon I was really struggling with writing a sermon to preach the following morning. I decided to gather my things and go out to the cemetery behind the property to sit in a tree to write. I went upstairs and splashed some water on my face in the bathroom, then shut off the light before venturing outside. Upon my return I couldn't help but stare in amazement as I rounded to the bottom of the stairs and saw that the bathroom light had come back on in my absence!

Though this was startling, it was nothing compared to one night later that fall. On this strange evening, I had decided to take a hot shower. The upstairs bathroom light is track lighting and it has a push and turn dial. I pushed the light on and turned the dial up, and then proceeded to shower. With the water running, I suddenly found myself in the dark behind the curtain. Anyone who has seen the movie *Psycho* knows that this is an uneasy situation in which to find oneself. I had to open the curtain and go to the switch on the wall to turn the lights back on. I pushed the dial. Nothing happened. Yet all the other lights in the house were still working. I pushed it again. Still no light appeared. To my surprise and horror I found that the dial had not been pushed off, just turned all the way down! Soaking wet, I patrolled upstairs and down to see if there was someone in the house, but found no one. I couldn't even hear a sound except that of the water running in the shower, beckoning my return. I finished that shower with my eyes and the curtain wide open!

I remember as a child the fascination I had for playing with light switches. When we die, perhaps that enthusiasm and pleasure returns. Or maybe it's just the easiest way to say hello.

Another series of startling occurrences commenced immediately upon my arrival in the home. I would awake each morning to find all the downstairs clocks stopped at 3:00 A.M. My mind raced for a logical explanation but, after days of taking out the batteries and putting the same ones back in only to then have the clocks begin working again, I began to believe that the only logical explanation was a supernatural one. None of these clocks were electrical and there was no way to keep them on time even though they were in three separate rooms: one in the sitting room, one in the living room, and one on the wall in the kitchen. Each one stopped at the exact same minute every night!

Suddenly one night the clocks just continued to run and the psychic activity seemed to stop.

Two years later, after I was married, one night my wife and I had drifted off to sleep in the quiet of our upstairs bedroom. We were awakened from our deep slumber by music playing and, slowly, we became consciously aware that someone had switched on our digital alarm clock resting on a table on the other side of the room. The alarm was still set for 6:00 A.M. When I got up and switched off the clock, I looked at it with amazement: it was three o' clock!

Between lights, clocks, and footsteps, in my early days at the parsonage I could find rest only by being in my bedroom with the window air conditioner on high and the alarm clock playing music so as to block out any disturbing bumps or noises. I could get the same effect in the sitting room downstairs by listening to the television or watching videos. In later years, my wife and I would achieve this effect by running two air purifiers in the home and, during the summer months, adding the additional insulation of fans and air conditioners. The noises of the home were effectively drowned out, though I am no longer gullible enough to believe that one can muffle all noises.

I remember a time in my home of origin that taught me this lesson. It started in a strange way. We had a kitchen light that would be left on in the evening when no one was home. One day it began to turn off on its own, then on again—and even do it several times in one evening. This continued for a while. It was late in an evening during this time that I came home to an empty house, locked the door, and went upstairs to take a shower. As I was under the shower with the water running, I suddenly heard the sound of the back door unlocking downstairs—which was unusual because normally the sound of the running water drowned out all the other sounds in the house. Grabbing a towel I quickly ran out of the bathroom and down the steps. To my horror, the door I had locked was standing open. I found no one in the house and could gain no explanation as to how the latched door had opened, or to how I could have heard it happen.

Similarly, one night in August 1996, my mufflers actively in place, I was startled awake moments before the sleep function of my clock ceased and the music grew quiet. At the other end of the hall, on the stairway to the third floor, despite the noise from the air conditioner, I could hear the sound of footsteps descending the stairs very slowly. I listened and, as before, they stopped inside the door at the bottom of the stairs. The house grew quiet. I closed my bedroom door and struggled to sleep again, saying prayers into the room and covering my head with the sheets.

The startling effect of this experience was soon forgotten however, when a new sound began to trouble me. For several days I began to experiment with turning off the radio to fall asleep. To my amazement, on the nights I did not run the air conditioner, I would hear the sounds of furniture moving in the room above me on the third floor. However, the scuffling could not be explained because the floor space right above me was only part of a room and mostly a cubby area where furniture just wouldn't fit. But even if furniture could fit along the wall outside the cubby space and in the room beside it, that still would not account for the sounds. The entire third floor was empty and the area above me was covered in carpet!

Despite the lack of a logical explanation, I soon found that the sound of things moving around on the third floor was nothing unusual. Sounds seemed to come from that part of the house with apparently no reasonable source.

One night two years later, my wife and I again lay down to sleep in our bedroom, only to be startled by the sound of a basketball, or a ball of some type, being bounced on the third floor.

Just to be sure it wasn't in our heads, we turned to each other and said, "Did you hear that?"

"Yes," came the mutual replies.

"Oh good," was our relieved and yet uneasy response to one another.

In time, we fell asleep.

Rocking in the Gray Morn

Living in a haunted house for me meant some radical changes in my hobbies. I grew up as a fan of books and movies in the genres of horror, true crime, and mystery thrillers. After a few weeks in Riegelsville, truth became harder to swallow and scarier than any fictional work in many respects. There's a big difference between watching or reading a scary story, and potentially living one. Wondering what is going to happen on any given night can be a captivating experience. In fact, living with the supernatural is much more interesting and enthralling than any book or movie could ever be.

My first months in the parsonage were filled with the daily experiences typical of many stories of haunting. Lights would suddenly turn themselves on or off; doors would open and close; and footsteps would echo throughout the house—though in each case these things happened when no one was around. That soon changed.

August 8,1996, began as a cold and dreary summer morning. The misty haze and fog rolling off the Delaware River had blanketed this small community by the time I climbed out of bed to begin another day at the church. I went to the window and lifted its shade to see the sun struggling to bring light and warmth to the cold of the morning air. Sleepily then, I emerged from my bedroom around 7 A.M. and began my trek downstairs to feed the cats and get some breakfast.

The gray of the morning cast a dim light into the foyer of the house as I started working my way down the stairs. Almost three quarters of the way down however, I felt as if my heart stopped as I took in the vision before me. In fact I had to blink my eyes several times to be sure what I was seeing was real. In the sitting room at the bottom of the stairs, just barely visible, I could see the back rails of my antique rocking chair moving as if someone was sitting on it, perhaps enjoying the quiet of the morning and relaxing before a hard day's work! The cats were with me on the stairs and I watched as the hair on their backs stood up as they apparently began seeing what I saw.

There was a moment of hesitation as I tried to decide what to do.

I called out, "Hello."

No response.

The silence was broken only by the sound of the creaking of the floorboards caused by the continued rocking of the chair rails.

I took a deep breath and slowly, ever so slowly, turned and decided to go back to bed for a little more rest.

My mind was spinning as I recalled many of the stories my predecessor had told of reading the newspaper on a rocking chair by the fireplace and then going to bed, only to find in the morning that the rocking chair was turned through the night and the newspapers obviously shuffled about.

That day I vowed that, until the time I moved out of the parsonage, rocking chairs would not sit in the foyer or within eyesight at the bottom of the steps. Since the time of our marriage however, my wife and I have had rocking chairs in the foyer, in the fireplace room, and in the sitting room. To my knowledge, none of the chairs have been seen to move by themselves again.

But I always watch them out of the corner of my eye. Who knows if someday they'll begin to rock on their own once more?

Cool Breeze on My Shoulder

I remember being taught in elementary school about the five senses of the body: the ability to hear, to see, to touch, to taste, and to smell. These are elements of our mortal life that allow us to enjoy and understand the world around us. In the spiritual realm, perhaps we retain our abilities to use these five senses. Perhaps the veil separating the spiritual realm from our mortal lives can be pulled back at times, allowing the spirits to see, smell, hear, and touch us.

It would seem to me from my combined experiences of the unknown shared in Riegelsville, that this assumption must indeed be true. Obviously the spirit in the parsonage was able to sense my presence and perhaps it was even able to see and hear me in my daily living. I know I have been able to see and hear its presence. I've even been able to feel it.

The morning of July 29, 1996, was the start of the last two days of my vacation before beginning my pastoral duties at St. John. On that day, I was intent on finishing the final pieces of moving in and I ventured to the third floor to clean the empty rooms of three years' worth of dead flies, bees, cobwebs, and dust.

I began vacuuming in the largest of the spaces and some half hour later, with sweat blinding me due to the stifling heat, I managed to work my way to the last of the empty rooms. I found myself vacuuming windowsills in a room that had obviously been unused for a long time. It stored some old doors and an antenna that a previous pastor had installed inside for some strange reason. Looking up at the open rafters and the immense amount of dirt, I made the conscious effort to dig in and get finished as soon as possible.

The heat of the day was unbearable, making my desire to complete the job grow stronger. As I was vacuuming one windowsill, with no air stirring on the third floor and the hot exhaust from the Shopvac making the air even more stifling, I sensed a cold breeze move slowly across my neck such that it made my hair rise. Almost immediately along with that tingling feeling came the sense of a presence there in the room with me.

Many times while cutting the lawn and riding the tractor in the yard, I had felt the discomfort of being watched through these windows. Now my discomfort felt confirmed, and was growing.

I quickly shut off the vacuum and looked around. Without surprise, there was no one to be seen. The moment seemed suspended in time. I watched, waiting, while the contrast of heat and cold caused all my muscles to tense and my eyes to focus. I was anxious to see whatever it was that had caused my unease. After a time the coldness subsided and, with no further unusual activity, I unplugged the vacuum and headed downstairs.

I soon learned that my "over the shoulder" experiences, as I would like to refer to them, would continue. In particular, they were frequent in an upstairs bedroom that I used for exercise and to practice my trumpet.

It was there on a summer afternoon that I was sitting in front of a window with the horn, using the sill as a music stand, and playing a hymn. I don't remember what the hymn was that I was practicing but, when the blare of the trumpet stopped and silence settled into the room, something strange happened. Slowly, I became aware that over my right shoulder, just above audible level, someone or something was humming music, and an unfamiliar tune at that!

I listened for a few moments, uncertain as to whether it was a vibration from the horn, or a real sound coming from some external source. I clamped my hand over the bell of the trumpet and rested it against my body to end whatever vibrations may have been there, but the humming continued. Next I got up and looked out the screen windows to see if, within earshot, there were any ice cream trucks playing music to call customers or any group of kids with a radio nearby. I saw and heard nothing outside.

Finally the silence returned and I began practicing my music again, this time resolving to stop halfway through and trick whoever the mysterious musician might be. I did just that and within seconds a faint humming began over my shoulder once more—in a tune that to this day I do not recognize. It sounded like an old hymn, but was very unfamiliar to me. Needless to say, my practice was cut short that afternoon.

Fortunately these experiences have not stopped me from practicing my instrument, nor have they deterred me from my love of music. To this day I still enjoy playing instruments, and have since taken up the guitar.

I read a story once about a man who played guitar one night while staying at a haunted inn. When he was finished playing, he was startled by the applause of some disembodied spectator. One can be sure that if that experience ever happens in Riegelsville, my music playing days will be short-lived.

A Ghostly Commentary

Lately it seems that every time we turn around there is a new "trial of the century" happening somewhere in the United States. From the Peterson murders to the Jackson scandal, people are talking about these high profile trials. It's funny because it wasn't very long ago when "the trial" everyone talked about as if it was the most important to thing to ever happen was O. J. Simpson's double homicide case. In the 1990s the event seemed to captivate the nation. Even now the story is referred to on many talk shows as, if not the trial of the century, then the trial of the nineties. This court fiasco electrified the country for over a year until a jury of his peers judged Simpson "not guilty."

However, it wasn't long before the ghost of the accusation haunted him again and a civil case was launched naming him as the defendant. In fall 1996, this trial drew to a close.

On the evening that the jury returned its verdict, I arrived home from a church meeting just as dusk was passing into night. Entering the darkened house, I turned on a few lights, then went around and closed all the blinds and shades as I normally did, and as many people do in the evening, to gain some privacy.

Finally I sat down to relax and turned on the television to see what was happening in the world. Of course what was happening was a media circus with various reporters intent on being the first folks to break the Simpson civil verdict to the waiting public. As I had followed the trial, I decided to listen and watch as the time counted down and the media began to report the results as if it was a sporting event.

41

Just as the first part of the verdict was spoken, "Guilty," I was startled by the sound of a shade snapping in another room. Now, knowing full well that it takes a hand to snap those shades, I got up to investigate. Gingerly stepping out of the sitting room and into the living room, I was comforted to find that the shades and blinds were closed tight and just as I had left them. When I came into the foyer however, I noticed the shade on the door to the side porch resting perfectly at half the length of the window.

The rest of the verdict could be overheard coming from the sitting room: "Guilty on all counts."

Could it be that my ghost was offering commentary on the verdict and celebrating justice being done? Was it finding unity with Nicole Brown and Ron Goldman? Maybe it was. For if indeed the spirit in the parsonage is that of Mary Louisa, she knows the pain of having one's young life cut short by circumstances out of their control. It would make sense that her ghost would be satisfied that someone was held accountable for this other life shortened before its natural span had ended. Who knows?

Maybe the spirit was just jealous that my attention had been drawn elsewhere and I wasn't thinking about its presence that evening.

To this day that shade has not moved in such a way again. Our upstairs shades however, have been known to, on occasion, rise up as if pulled by some unseen hand.

But if the movement of shades isn't enough to get our attention, then perhaps our ghost likes to be sure it accomplishes that task. Playing with doors is a great way to do this!

In December 2000, my parents and aunt and uncle came to dinner at our house to celebrate the Christmas season. Before dinner, my mother and I stood in conversation in a hallway just inside the closed door off our back porch. All of a sudden I noticed the knob of the door turn and saw it swing open. I took a deep breath and casually closed the door with some nonchalant expression. My mother made no comment, but kind of laughed it off when I told her what I had seen.

This same event had occurred weeks before as several guests were preparing to leave a Christmas party my wife and I had hosted in our home. Just inside the door, our friends stood talking with us as we kept the conversation going in one of those long drawn out goodbyes. Suddenly, the door to the porch swung open. No one was behind it. Was the spirit growing impatient and telling us it was time for our guests to leave? Perhaps.

It seems that the ghost getting one's attention with doors might be something that has a bit of history in the parsonage. One afternoon in 2004, I was at the post office getting mail when a woman approached me and asked about the ghost stories I had been collecting from town. Our conversation moved through some of the stories in this book and then settled on stories of my home. In the midst of our conversation, the woman with whom I was speaking shared with me that a previous pastor had installed multiple locks on almost every door in the parsonage. It seemed to me that she felt he was afraid for some reason. Judging by my experiences, the locks may have been for peace of mind—maybe to keep those pesky doors closed!

Why the use of doors to get one's attention? That I cannot answer. But I do believe that spirits often attempt to communicate with us and this is one way to do it. It also seems, at times, that when a door opening isn't subtle enough, then the spirits have even more emphatic ways to speak.

In fall 1996, I had finally gathered the nerve to finish cleaning the third floor room that I had hastily abandoned weeks before after my strange "over the shoulder" experience. With that work done, the room was ready to be used; only I didn't have the courage to actually put anything up there.

One Friday night, my mother came to stay with me in order to attend a church event the following morning. As we got ready to go to bed, I called down the hall to her and asked if she would go up to the third floor to see the job I had done in cleaning. She left the bedroom at the front of the house and went upstairs while I was busy in my bedroom.

A few moments later I heard her calling me to come upstairs. Expecting some pointers on how I might clean the rooms better, I went to the bottom of the steps and found her standing at the top on the third floor.

"Do you know if the electricity is okay up here?" she asked.

I responded that it had all been checked over prior to my moving in and that I thought some wiring had even been replaced.

The answer seemed to surprise her. She then shared that the lights up there had brightened and dimmed, then brightened and dimmed again while she stood in the carpeted bedroom above.

As we spoke the lights brightened and dimmed a third time, this time at the top of the stairs in the third floor hallway. I had never seen this happen and have experienced it myself only a few times since. My wife says that she too has had this experience.

Is this an attempt at emphatic ghostly communication?

Are there even more emphatic attempts?

One of my more interesting experiences would lead me to believe that the answer is "yes." I base this on an event that happened in the fall of 1996.

In mid-November a friend came to stay with me for a time. One afternoon he had planned to be away but, before he left, I got up the courage to take advantage of his presence at that moment and, with an added sense of security that someone else was in the house, I set about emptying the middle bedroom on the second floor and transporting all of its stored items up to the third floor room with carpeting and electricity. Being the middle of the afternoon, thoughts of ghosts or mischief were the furthest from my mind. As I began my first trip up the stairs, my friend left the house.

Now up until this time, I was afraid to use the third floor and had absolutely forbidden my cats from venturing up there. But on this day, as I started up the steps, my black cat, Nightshade, tore past me and up to the third floor where she began running around. As is usually the case, my long-haired cat, Evening, followed her slowly and began to explore as well. She was content to run around in a long room to the left at the top of the stairs while Nightshade seemed to be drawn toward the door of the carpeted room. I carried a small box in my hands and crossed the threshold of this room, placing the box on the floor in the room's far corner.

As I left to get another box, I passed Nightshade sitting in the doorway hissing and crying and staring into the room. I laughed to myself that she was crazy and came downstairs. Maybe she was crazy, or more likely, spooked. Before I was able to pick up another box, I heard what sounded like the slamming of a foot against the floor coming from the room upstairs that I had just left. Within seconds, Nightshade leaped down the steps and dived under a twin bed in the front bedroom; her claws digging into the hardwood floor, her body shivering. I yelled out to whatever could hear that it should stop bothering my cats and charged up with another box to share some choice words with this unseen phantom. It was as if whatever was in the room that day didn't want the cats around and was saying, "Scat, cat!" Needless to say, it took quite a while for Nightshade to travel up there again.

Soon after, I noticed that the threshold of that room often set the cats to hissing. I have witnessed this behavior several times and when these experiences occur, the cats will usually only enter the room if I go first and they leave when I do.

With seemingly so much commentary, our ghost could probably write its own editorial page…

Men's Voices

When I was a young child, we had many kids in our neighborhood who would stay out late at night. From the screens in my bedroom windows, occasionally a conversation would float through the air and reach my hearing as I lay in bed. The voices would last only a fleeting moment and sound like just a murmur. The same could be said of the people who would walk on our street; from whom you would hear pieces of words and the sounds of conversation as they talked and walked together on their way past our house. I am sure this is an experience that is quite common to many people.

In the days not too far past, it was not uncommon for folks to gather on the porches of homes and spend hours in conversation—sometimes into the deepest parts of the evening and long into the darkest hours of night. Their murmurs could be heard in homes nearby and within the house of the porch on which they sat.

Several times since moving to Riegelsville, the sounds of disembodied conversations seemed to echo in the kitchen and side porch areas of the parsonage. I was first aware of these sounds in the silence of the night about six months after moving in. They would become audible *only* in the silence, and then just above a noise level that could be detected, almost like what is known as white noise. In fact, one might describe the voices as a whispering conversation—definitely bass in tone with the occasional high-pitched sound.

My tendency was to ignore them though, because the house across the street was undergoing a massive reconstruction due to a structure fire and there was a constant flow of workers and caretakers coming and going from the house at all hours. I was convinced that what I was hearing at night was the same murmurs and conversation bits that I had heard as a child, this time from the many construction workers across the street.

Yet the sounds continued at the same audible level even as fall turned to winter and the screened windows were replaced with glass. Then the construction project moved to within the walls of our neighboring home and the late night traffic around the house yielded to an empty driveway through the hours of darkness. The sounds still continued.

One night in November or early December 1996, a friend of mine was alone in the parsonage while I led a retreat for high school students in our church social room. About 11:30 P.M., a knock on the social room windows startled us in the midst of our activities. It was my friend looking very excited. He anxiously asked if we would unlock the door for him, which we did. Excitedly, he came in and explained that he had heard men talking in the parsonage and had quickly left so that he wouldn't be alone.

I asked if he had locked the door and he said, "No."

I sent him home to lock the door, and tried to make light of his experience so as not to frighten him more. But I did share with him that this incident had occurred before and was ghostly in origin.

As time passed, occasionally I would still hear those phantom sounds in the parsonage when I was up on the second floor or down in the kitchen area. They became common, and I began to get used to them.

In June of that year I met my future wife and, upon our marriage later that year, we began sleeping in the same bedroom that I had been using at the back of the house. Several mornings she would tell me that through the night she had heard voices, deep in tone and most likely male, murmuring down in the kitchen area of the house. She was unable to make out what they were saying, but was sure it was people talking.

To this day, she describes the sounds as that of two people walking down the street with their conversation growing louder as they approach and softer as they go past—people engaged in conversation where there are no people. She also describes it as overhearing folks sitting on their porch and talking lightly about the events of the day—relaxing or having fun.

In early 1998, we moved our bedroom and have not since slept in that previous room. That room is now a guest room and is mostly unused, except for storage or the occasional cat that wanders in for a nocturnal rest. Do you suppose cats can hear the ghostly conversation? Maybe they can understand.

A Face in the Window

Sometime in October 1996, I found myself struggling to keep up my energy between the experiences I was having at home and the stresses of church ministry. Friends recommended that I try a diet and exercise program and so, after getting some equipment, I began a rigorous program of 90-minute daily workouts in the second floor room where I had experienced the humming over my shoulder.

I tried to exercise in mid-afternoon every day. As it happened, one day I had missed my workout and decided that I would try it in the evening. About 45 minutes into my exercises that night, I began weight lifting. Nothing seemed unusual until I began to lift the weights while facing out one of the upstairs windows.

Suddenly, as I stood up, sweat pouring from my face and barbell in hand, I found myself staring in shock at a reflection in the window before me. There, standing behind my right shoulder, I saw the image of a man. He was slightly taller than myself and mostly in shadow, his features indistinguishable. He was silent. The only noise in the room was a CD playing and my cry of fright. Startled, I dropped the barbell and turned, but no one was there.

I can say that the event terrified me. To this day, when I enter that room in the evening to pull down the shades, my heart skips a beat as I look into the reflection in the panes—wondering if that visitor will ever return again.

Footsteps Yet Again

One evening, a friend and I sat in deep conversation in the sitting room on the first floor of the parsonage. This was several weeks after my encounter with the mysterious man reflected in an upstairs window.

Suddenly we were startled to hear the sounds of someone walking on the floorboards in the bedroom above us—the room my friend was occupying at the time. With a look to each other and a casual comment, we acknowledged that something was up there, but neither one of us decided to go and seek out the source of the noises.

It was one of the only times this friend ever acknowledged the spirit's presence. Another occasion when he did speak of it was one afternoon as he told me a tale that sounded familiar to my own experiences. It seemed that he was tired because he hadn't gotten much sleep the night before. Now I hadn't noticed any noises in the house that night and had slept well, so I was curious as to his inability to sleep and inquired why. It was clear he did not want to talk about it in detail and we ended the conversation. What he didn't say led me to believe that he had heard something unusual.

Whistling was a part of this friend's life and routine. He would whistle occasionally on his way in or out of the house. One night after his visit had ended, I went to bed and was starting to fall asleep when I became aware of whistling in the hallway downstairs. The tune was the same one my friend had often whistled but I heard no footsteps, was aware that no door had opened, and what's more, my friend no longer had his keys.

Perhaps the ghost had grown fond of him and was whistling a tribute to say goodbye. I can only say that the whistling has not happened since.

The footsteps however, have continued sporadically over the years.

In late spring 2004, as I was working on the revisions for this manuscript, I was startled one afternoon by a loud noise upstairs and the sound of someone walking. When my wife arrived home, I ventured up to the second floor to see what had happened and discovered that the front bedroom door at the bottom of the third floor staircase had opened. Apparently the spirit may have been curious and may have been seeking to get closer to me as I was typing out its stories.

Henry's Nose

Anyone who has read ghost stories knows that some ghosts are silent, others are playful, and some are mischievous.

When I was in high school I had a friend who claimed a spirit she had dislodged from her *Ouija* board would hide things on members of the family and turn around the furniture in rooms. I have also heard stories of ghosts stacking up all the dishes on kitchen counters or tables while the homeowners slept.

"Louisa," if that is indeed our spirit, seems to have a bit of a mischievous side as well. In this case, her playfulness revolved around her husband George. It's also possible though, that the spirit at work in this story is that of the man I saw reflected in that upstairs window while exercising—maybe it's even George!

When I was a child, my brother spent a great deal of time learning performance magic. Through him, I happened upon the presentation art of ventriloquism and dabbled with it using a dummy purchased from one of those holiday catalogs. Upon graduating from college, I bought a semi-professional dummy and named him Noah, but still was not happy because he didn't have all the functions I had seen in professional puppets. Thus, upon coming to Riegelsville, I promised myself I would fulfill my desire to have a professional puppet—and even better I would build it myself.

I purchased plans and labored long to build a workbench and get the supplies I needed. Determining that upstairs was the most comfortable place for me to work, I set about building my puppet in a room on the second floor. I converted my former storage room to a work center and spent long evenings there following meetings at the church.

Building the puppet was really enjoyable and psychically uneventful until mid-March 1997. Around that time, I began to shape the nose that my figure would wear. With plastic wood and my fingers, I built up a nose that I hoped would be round and bulbous in the shape of a stereotypical clown or comedian. The directions said the plastic wood should dry for 24 hours so, content with my work, I set it to form and retired for the night.

The next morning I entered my workroom and found that when the nose had hardened it was no longer bulbous and round, but had taken on the appearance of an older nose—droopy on the sides and flat in the front. There was no evidence that its change was due to poor positioning or gravity. I grew disappointed... and curious. Though I was making an old man puppet, I wanted it to have the bulbous nose of comedy. So I set about building it up again—this time laying the head flat to dry so that gravity could not affect it.

For two days the nose continued to change overnight into exactly the same droopy shape and nothing seemed to prevent it. Coincidentally on one of those days, I picked up B. F. Fackenthal's history of St. John Church while working at the office and began to flip through it. There I was startled to see a picture of the Rev. George Aughinbaugh as an older man. His nose looked exactly like that of my puppet!

That evening, I determined to change both noses. I shaped a nose that was a combination of the nose in the book and the bulbous nose I desired. That one seemed to be agreed upon by all of us in the house—for it stayed as I had left it. I've never heard of artistic ghosts and I'm not sure if someone was trying to communicate with me, but that experience was a curious one which I shall never forget each time I pick up that puppet and behold his face!

The Evil One

One unique experience I had when I was a teenager was the opportunity to listen to a series of lectures by Ed and Lorraine Warren, famous psychics and ghost hunters extraordinaire. They had investigated incidents in Amityville, New York; West Pittston, Pennsylvania; and multiple castles overseas, and they had come to Jim Thorpe, Pennsylvania, to show many of their pictures, discuss their investigations, and even talk about exorcisms—a highlight topic of the lecture series.

During their presentations, one night they brought in a priest to bless the crowd and then played the tape of an actual exorcism they had witnessed. The voice of the evil spirit on the tape was hideous and so unnerving that words cannot do it justice. It made the hair stand up on the back of my neck and was enough to make my heart stop beating.

I had not seen the classic horror flick *The Exorcist* at that time but, since viewing the film, I have come to relate the voice of the demon in that movie as similar to the one I heard on their exorcism tape. The sound of that voice still sends chills through me as I recall it even today. I remember going home from the Warren lecture that night and wishing to never hear that voice again.

Many years later, in April 1997, that incident was the furthest thing from my mind as I rested while getting over a bout of sickness. It was dusk, and I had decided to lie down to read and watch television before going to sleep. Snuggle, my youngest cat, curled up beside me on the bed. I read for a while, until the words on the page began to dance and run together, and soon I drifted off to a deep sleep listening to the music of MTV.

Suddenly, my rest was broken by a gruff, unnerving voice that yelled loudly into the room and said my name.

"Jeffrey!" It said.

My eyes snapped open and I looked to the doorway from where the sound had emanated—it was the door to the hall. The first sensation I recall having when fully awake, was that of an electrical, negative energy pouring into the room. It grew bitter cold. Glancing at the cat, it was evident that she too had heard the voice, for her hair was on end and she was staring wide-eyed into the hall and hissing. I remember saying a prayer under my breath and then getting out of bed and moving quickly to the door to examine the hallway for the source of the voice. It was empty.

After composing myself, I walked around the upstairs and found nothing disturbed. Soon after, I returned to my bed, turned off the television, and clicked on the radio. That night I slept with the light on and the door closed until the morning sunlight cast an orange glow of warmth into the room.

Seven years later, I found myself no longer thinking about that voice when I walked around at night through the second and third floors of the parsonage.

Then one evening in late winter or early spring, my wife and I had been out for a time and had come home exhausted. We retired to bed and our two dogs curled up on the covers beside us. Sleep came easily.

About three in the morning I was awakened by a scream from my wife as she jumped out of bed and ran toward the door of the room. Trying to comprehend what was happening, I asked her what was wrong.

"Someone was whispering in my ear," she excitedly said.

She then described that as she was lying in bed on her side, deep in sleep, she suddenly began to sense a presence leaning over her and felt a cold breeze drift by her head. Then, as she described it, a hoarse, cold, unnerving voice spoke to her saying, "I still remember...."

The meaning of those words remains unclear to this day.

This incident was truly disturbing to me because my wife is not prone to remembering dreams. In fact, I can't recall one time in our six years of marriage that she told me about a dream she had experienced. I have no doubt that her encounter was real. Perhaps more unnerving for me is that the voice she described sounded eerily like the voice I had heard years before; and like that on the Warren's tape.

Sleep was sporadic for us the rest of that night.

Married Haunting

My family used to tease me about how hard it would be to find someone who would marry me and live in a haunted house. In June 1997, I was blessed to find Stephanie who, six months later, became my wife.

One evening in late summer 1997, as she and I stood at the top of the second floor stairs discussing plans for her move to Riegelsville, we suddenly heard the sound of something falling down the staircase from the third floor. The sound was similar to what one would expect from a body tumbling down the steps and crashing into the walls and door yet, when the door was opened, nothing could be found inside to have caused the noise.

Throughout the months following our marriage, Stephanie would regularly comment on hearing voices in the kitchen late at night. Even after years had passed and I began to callously say that I hadn't heard or experienced anything weird (thus I was thinking the spirits had left and we were alone in the house again), she would assure me that she still sensed there was something present with us.

Sometimes the sensation that the ghost was near was stronger than at other times. Occasionally, I would feel as if someone was present and visible, clearly seen when viewed out of the corner of my eye. At other times we would simply share a nagging feeling that we were being watched. The experience was enough to ward Stephanie off from entering the third floor or the basement unless we were together.

On one night in particular, our ghost made its presence known quite clearly. There was a picture that we had hung on the downstairs hallway wall. Exactly what the picture depicted, I cannot recall, but I do remember that I used to tease my wife that I didn't like it.

Late on this night we had fallen into a deep sleep. As had happened before in the parsonage, suddenly I was awakened by a loud noise but my wife didn't seem to have heard it. It sounded like a large bang echoing through the house.

Sitting up, I quickly put on my robe and entered the hallway to find the cats randomly seated in different places.

Earlier that day, I had been on the third floor and had left the door open at the bottom of those stairs. Now Nightshade was seated at the bottom of the third floor steps meowing and looking down the hallway toward the landing on which I stood. I looked down the stairs to the first floor and could see Evening sitting halfway down the steps meowing and staring into the sitting room, now converted to a double office. Snuggle sat in the hallway on the first floor looking into the office and meowing.

Turning on the light, I felt what I could only describe as a weird sensation. It was as if the hallway was a vacuum and no sound could be heard other than an occasional meow from one of the cats. I'm not sure if it was adrenaline, sleepiness, or something else, but the feeling was unnerving.

I descended the stairs and quickly looked at the windows in the living room and dining room to find that they were intact. Next I glanced into the office to see if the cats were meowing at some obvious person or thing, but saw nothing unusual. Finally, I turned and stared down the first floor hallway. To my surprise, the picture that had been hanging on the hallway wall was lying, face down, on the floor. Its perimeter was perfectly set within the parallel lines of the floorboards and it was square in the middle of the hall. In fact, it was so perfect that I don't think I could have placed it there myself by sliding it off the hook and letting it fall. I got chills and quickly picked it up and leaned it against the wall before hurrying back to bed.

The next day, we examined the situation more closely. My wife believed that the picture had vibrated off its hook as the house rattled from the trucks traveling Route 611 some 50 yards away. I believe there is a supernatural explanation to the activity because, to the time of this writing, no other picture has vibrated off that same hook or any other hook in the house.

Hearing the Stories

The coupling of being a parish minister and living in a haunted home has created some unique experiences in, and of, itself.

Early in my ministry, I was making my first pastoral call to a family in the church when, toward the close of my visit, the wife of the couple asked me, "How is the lady in your house?"

"Excuse me?" I remember replying. At this time I was a bachelor and the question caught me off guard, leading me to wonder what rumors she was hearing.

"You know, the ghost," she said.

"Oh," was all I could manage. "She's okay."

Having the question asked really took me by surprise.

Now the question no longer surprises me at all.

I remember another incident early in my ministry where one September day I had gone into a flower shop downtown to pick up a bouquet. As the flowers were prepared, a member of the church, whom I hadn't yet met, asked me about my ghost.

She then proceeded to tell me that some people claim to have seen "Louisa" walking in the cemetery near her prominent gravestone.

There is also the story told to me in summer 1997 by a young mother. Her son had run home one night the week before because he had seen a light moving around in the third floor of the church office building. It seemed as if someone was moving from room to room, but the building was totally dark and closed up for the day!

Indeed, parishioners and friends often ask us for stories of our ghost, or tell us stories of their own—as do perfect strangers.

One of these encounters happened at the town post office when I was picking up our mail.

A woman stopped and inquisitively asked, "Are you the new pastor in town?"

Now, I had been in Riegelsville over three years by then, so I replied, "Yes, I guess you could say that."

"It's a nice church," she said.

I agreed and began sorting my mail as she went out to her car. I then proceeded to my vehicle only to see her stop and backtrack.

"Can I ask you a question?" she again inquired.

"Sure," I said. "Though I may not have the answer."

"Is your house haunted?" came the wide-eyed question.

I laughed and said, "What makes you ask that?"

"I have heard stories," she replied.

"That's funny, I've heard them too." I said.

And with that I began a conversation with a perfect stranger.

Now, I had often read about and heard people share the fact that if you want to hear someone else's stories about anything in life, simply engage in similar activities with them.

Have a baby, and you'll hear countless baby stories.

Buy a car, and you'll hear everyone's car stories.

Experience a ghost, and suddenly you're a safe person with whom others can confide their strange experiences.

I was attending a funeral luncheon one day when I was asked about the ghost in the parsonage. After sharing a tale or two, a town businessman inquired as to whether I really believed in ghosts.

I said, "Yes."

He began to share with me stories from his building, which I share with you later in this text.

And then there are tales that are learned in the course of ministry itself.

One evening I met with a young couple that was planning to be married in one of the homes along "Mansion Row." We sat in a large room on the first floor of the house as we talked over the details of the ceremony and learned more about one another.

Throughout the time we were together however, my eyes kept getting drawn to a wall-sized mirror in the hallway just outside the room.

Finally, I could resist no longer and asked, "Do you have any ghosts in this house?"

I believe their response was, "No. Not really."

I then explained about the attraction of that mirror to me and, to my surprise, they shared that their dog couldn't go past that mirror without acting very strange around it.

The soon-to-be husband then shared with me that though there weren't any ghosts in the house that he was aware of, there had been a suicide in the building at one point in its history.

He then asked, "Would you like a tour?"

I eagerly said, "Yes."

We traveled throughout the first floor of the house with nothing unusual to speak about.

Upstairs however, was a different experience for me. We moved through a hallway and approached one room toward the back of the house. As the young couple entered the room, they began showing me different aspects of it.

But their words were lost on me because as I crossed the threshold of the space, I felt as if an electrical current went through me and my legs were cut out from under me. I braced myself on the doorframe and tried to catch my breath.

They noticed and asked, "Are you okay?"

I explained what I had experienced.

"You're good," the man said. "This is the room where the suicide occurred."

One learns that there are also tales told that tie the unexplainable experiences of the present with history.

The story is shared of a building in town into which a woman had moved her residence. Soon she was in the process of unpacking and had many boxes to go through.

As the tale was told to me, this new homeowner put the boxes in the basement and, while she was there, discovered an old tool that had been left behind by the previous owners.

Curious about it, but not paying much attention, she left the tool downstairs and took a carton upstairs to unpack. She took various items out of the box and placed them around the home only to discover, when she returned to the box sometime later, that the old tool had appeared near the empty carton.

She carried it back downstairs and put it on a shelf, then took another carton. Again, after unpacking that carton, she returned to find the strange tool sitting next to the empty box. It was as if it wanted to tell her a story from the past.

As I was told the tale, she then took the tool down to the basement and placed it in a cabinet. Again she took a box to empty, and again the tool traveled mysteriously to the first floor!

Finally, one tale published in the town library's Christmas House Tour booklet from years gone by, shares that the old parsonage of the Lutheran church also allegedly has a spirit that walks its stairs. The present owners say that they have had no supernatural experiences.

The Figure in Black

To the average person, there may be no experience more startling than seeing something moving about in your home in the middle of the night.

One Saturday evening, my wife and I had retired to our bedroom for a much needed rest. Early on Sunday morning, while it was still dark, my wife arose and left our bedroom quietly. I don't remember much about her leaving the room except that it seemed just seconds before she rushed back in and closed the door.

"I think I just saw our ghost," she excitedly said.

I remember being at once scared and curious.

"What did you see?" I asked.

"I don't want to talk about it," came the reply. "Go and check it out."

She got back in bed quickly and took a deep breath.

This was almost funny for me, but frightening too.

For weeks we had not seen or heard anything unusual in the house and I was beginning to believe that our spirit had moved along to another place. Now, tentatively, I got up and put on my robe, then slowly entered the hall and walked to the landing to investigate this alleged phantom.

As I stepped out onto the landing, instantaneously, out of the corner of my eye, I saw a shadow, about six feet tall with clearly visible legs and a head, swiftly cross the foyer on the first floor. It traveled from right to left and disappeared into the office below. Dumbstruck, I stood and looked down into the foyer, listening to a lone cat's meow. Then I walked across the hall and back again trying to retrace my steps to make the shadow return, hoping to explain what I had seen. Try as I might however, even with the bathroom light for help, I could not cause the shadow to reappear. My heart began to race and I quickly returned to bed.

I gave the explanation, "You must have seen a shadow."

It took a little while to get over such a curious sight. I wanted to know what my wife had seen, so I asked her, but she said she didn't want to talk about it. We eventually did get back to sleep.

When morning came, we spoke nothing of the previous night's incident. Both of us finished our morning routines and left for our respective churches to lead worship. My wife's ministry at that time kept her away from home most of Sunday so, eager to talk about what happened, I told some parishioners my tale from the night before.

The day passed quickly and it wasn't long before the afternoon sun turned to evening dusk once again. My wife and I met at the home of some good friends with whom we planned to share dinner.

As we ate and enjoyed our time together, my wife began to share her experience of the night before. She told the story of entering the hallway from our bedroom and stepping out onto the landing. There, below her, she saw a shadow about six feet tall, with discernable shoulders, move swiftly across the foyer from left to right.

The hair on the back of my neck stood up and I shared my experience of the exact same sighting. Only for me, the shadow had moved from the right to the left.

I sat there surprised to have my experience confirmed! We had not talked all day, yet now I heard what could have been my own story spoken from my wife's lips.

I have no doubt our experience was real because we both seemed shocked at one another's story. What was this shadowy shape? Was it a spirit or a visual trick?

If it was a visual trick, then why did we both experience it?

I believe that we shared a mutual sighting of our ghost on its evening rounds. I also have the feeling that the shape is the same one that I saw staring back at me over my shoulder in that upstairs exercise room those eighteen months before. No one really knows...

The Uninvited Guest

When I was growing up, I remember hearing people say that when you set a table for dinner you should always include an extra place setting in case you have an unexpected, uninvited, guest. My wife and I often bypass that extra place setting in our home because we have an uninvited guest at our gatherings on a regular basis—one that doesn't require dishes.

In the summer of 1998, we invited some close friends and colleagues to our home for a backyard picnic. By late afternoon we had grown comfortable, gathered in small groups around several picnic tables, and were actively conversing and catching up with one another. Time passed quickly as we enjoyed our meal and the company of good friends. In the background, the sound of the stereo playing emanated from inside the house and an occasional car traveled down the highway. Other than that, it was pretty quiet except for the random whine of a rogue cat at the screen door crying for a morsel to eat. Before long, the shadows lengthened into late evening.

Darkness descended upon us.

Suddenly, one colleague's wife pointed toward a window on the second floor of the parsonage and asked, "Is someone in the house? The lights just turned on upstairs."

Before my wife or I could reply, another friend very quickly stated, "Don't worry about it. They just turned off again."

We looked around and realized that no one had been in the house.

Late that year, we would come to recognize that the spirit in our home enjoyed being present for dinner parties.

Each year, my wife and I have hosted members of the church with an open house at the parsonage close to the Christmas holiday. This was to be our second gathering and I was helping to prepare for the event by baking a batch of my grandmother's peanut butter cookies.

I like to bake. Yet this recipe is an all-afternoon affair because it yields a batch of twenty dozen peanut butter cookies. By the time I am half through with baking them, I need a break.

It was just such a moment when I remember leaving the kitchen to enjoy some fresh, cool, air outside. As I re-entered the house off the driveway porch, I was suddenly overcome by the familiar sensation that I was being watched. This time it seemed to come from someone standing on the second floor landing at the bottom of the stairs to the third floor. It was as if the presence was looking down over the banister rail at the back doorway. This same area gave me chills when I first moved to the house because it always felt as if someone was watching you in this spot. It always made me feel vulnerable. Not only that, this spot where the presence now seemed to be (at the bottom of the third floor stairs looking over the railing) was the same spot where the disembodied footsteps had always ended for my predecessor. It was also the area where his son had seen a woman in old-fashioned dress.

With this familiar feeling upon me, I quickly turned my head and looked to the second floor. There I saw a dark, shadowy figure step away from the banister rail. It was only present for a fleeting moment and I know there was no one else in the house.

A few weeks after this experience, the day of our Open House arrived and our home was filled with old friends and new guests. In particular, on this day, I met a friend of my wife for the first time. In fact, she had brought her entire family to our party and my wife gave them the grand tour of every nook and cranny of our house. As the afternoon passed, they visited and spent time enjoying the food and fellowship.

About a month later, we had the occasion to be with these friends again. Shortly into our visit, they shared with us that their boys had felt strange in our home. It seemed they were spiritually sensitive to something there that didn't feel quite right, and the uncomfortable energy seemed to emanate from that room on the third floor where the footsteps had paced my first night in the house. In fact, the experience was so strong that the boys had said that they wouldn't like to visit our home at night.

One of these friends also told us that, later in the afternoon, she had observed the image of a woman, who was dressed in an older style, mingling among the guests in our home and moving from room to room. No one else seemed to notice this uninvited guest. Our friends had purposely spoken nothing about it until seeing us at this later time.

We have no reason to doubt their experience. Having come to know them over the years, these friends are not prone to fabricating stories.

Could it be that Louisa had been longing to celebrate Christmas once more and just couldn't resist the chance? Or maybe she was just lonely and wanted some company. Either way, she seems to feel invited to our parties—no matter what the occasion!

The Church Ghost

In the early days of Riegelsville's existence, the Riegel Paper Corporation was the focal point of this small community. In fact, the existence of the only two Protestant churches in town is due to the faith of the Riegel family.

The story, as I was told it, is that the Riegel family wanted to establish a place of worship for those who worked the mill. Thus, a union church was created in 1849. Within the next two decades, the congregation divided and the Reformed members of the parish laid the cornerstone for an edifice of their own in 1872. The congregation has worshipped in this building ever since. In 1957, the congregation voted to become part of the newly created United Church of Christ. It has served as a UCC congregation since that time.

Early in my career as pastor of St. John, I had a late evening planning meeting with a church member in the old Cyrus Stover home that now functions as our church office. That evening, as we left the building, a light caught my eye and I turned my head toward the church. There I saw, through a round window on the basement floor of the structure, the silhouette of a man wearing a derby and holding a lantern. Excitedly I spoke of the image, but the member did not seem to see it. However, they did accompany me on a search of the premises that, to my surprise, turned up nothing. In fact the window through which I had seen the gentleman was blocked on the inside by a cast iron stove. No one could have stood there!

70

As time has passed, I have come to find that several unexplainable, perhaps supernatural, experiences have taken place at the church.

One person tells the story of being alone in the social room at night and hearing a music box click on in the nursery at the rear of the room. Curious about the sound, they got up and went into that room and began to explore, only to find that there were no visible toys there that played music and nothing that would account for the sound. In fact, the tune stopped playing when they crossed the threshold. After returning to the social room and beginning their work one more time, the music box clicked on again. Very quickly they left the building.

There are other unexplainable sights and sounds as well. Some folks tell of being startled by hearing the heavy front door slam closed when no one is in the foyer of the church and the door hasn't visibly moved. Still others say that it is not unusual to hear the sound of the chair lift embarking on a ghostly glide up or down the stairs to the sanctuary—with no visible rider!

Perhaps these noises make more sense if one considers that they may come from the spirit of a woman who has been seen, and heard, in the building.

More than one person can attest to being startled by the sound of what seems like fabric brushing against itself as if a woman was walking by in an old Victorian dress. And perhaps most interesting of all is the alleged tale told by one faithful church worker about seeing a woman in the balcony—standing there or pacing. One choir member attests that once in a while she, too, thinks she has seen this woman from the corner of her eye—walking or standing in the balcony.

No matter what the stories of old, when someone wants to prove or disprove ghost stories, those that can be corroborated are the most enchanting and convincing.

For example, there are the unexplainable and corroborated happenings from December 1999 and January 2000. They coincide with events happening in our home during that same period of time—

Fig 4. St. John United Church of Christ—built in 1872.

a fact that leads me to believe that at least one of our spirits makes its way from building to building in an almost cyclic pattern.

In December 1999, church choir rehearsals moved from the social hall into the sanctuary on a Wednesday night. Immediately after this, strange phenomena began which some have tried to explain with electrical surges and others by human error.

For a period of six weeks at least, on Wednesday nights after choir rehearsal in the sanctuary and/or on Sunday evenings following morning worship, the electric chandeliers would unexplainably turn back on in the sanctuary of the church. Not only would they click on at their lowest settings, but also the dials that one has to turn to operate the lights would be stripped off their mechanisms. On at least two occasions the people that turned the lights off were very experienced in doing so.

On one evening during this time, I was taking trash from our home to the garage on the back of the parsonage property. Heading up the yard with the trash bag, I looked over to the church as always and noted that the building was normal——dark and resting after the typical Sunday schedule. I remember thinking nothing of it as I went into the garage and put down the garbage. When I stepped back out of the garage however, I was startled to see a faint glow of light now coming from the sanctuary of the church. I looked harder and could see that no cars were in the parking lot.

Now I grew a little nervous, but decided that I wasn't going to deal with it. I went in the house and called our property committee chairman to go and turn out the lights, but found to my chagrin that he wasn't home. So, reluctantly, I decided to shut them off myself.

As I drove over to the church, I watched the building to see if a prankster would be noted leaving by the doors or windows or if I could see any shapes of people moving about inside that might explain the lights. There was nothing.

Stepping out of the car in the cold winter air, it felt like I was standing before a mausoleum. My hands were shaking and my heart was pounding as I unlocked the heavy door and stepped inside. A musty and ominous feeling seemed to permeate the church.

Perhaps the feeling came from within myself, or maybe not, but it felt as if the air grew even colder as I climbed the steps in the dark to the second floor hallway above.

There, an eerie feeling that was compounded by the intense cold overwhelmed me. Forcing my feet to move, I walked to the middle of the hall and looked through the open double entry to behold an astounding sight. All of the chandeliers were turned on at just candlelight level. The room was cold and silent, and it reminded me quite clearly of a funeral parlor prepared for a wake.

I shouted something into the sanctuary about how unfunny this trick really was and then proceeded to shut off the lights. Without hesitation, I hurried back down the steps and left the building.

I would think that I was crazy, but some choir members also tell stories about those sanctuary lights. One couple shared with me that, on several occasions, they would attend rehearsal in the sanctuary and one of them would turn off the lights. Yet upon exiting the church and entering the parking lot, they would be startled to see that the sanctuary lights had turned back on again.

Over and over it happened.

Then one week the light show stopped just as suddenly as it had started.

Many months later, a church musician reported being alone in the sanctuary rehearsing a musical piece and being repeatedly disturbed by the sound of a person walking in the hall outside the sanctuary. Yet this person knew they were alone and the front door was locked

One particular encounter in the church building was a little frightening.

In June 2001, my wife and I adopted a Jack Russell Terrier.

One Sunday afternoon, we brought him to the church social room as we prepared a craft activity for the children of the vacation church school that was set to begin that night.

Jaxon ran about the social room as we worked, playing with his toys and sniffing all over. Suddenly he seemed drawn to the foyer of the building and, as he entered there, the hair on his back stood up and he began barking loudly.

Many attempts to quiet him later, I finally had to drag him outside to calm him down. After some time, we went back into the building and once more Jaxon played for a while until he seemed drawn to the foyer again. This time, he sniffed about until he reached the bottom of the stairs to the sanctuary.

Suddenly he once more began barking, hair on end, at what seemed to be something on the stairs.

I dragged him back into the social room yet again and watched. It seemed, even with the doors closed, that he kept being drawn to the foyer. Finally, I propped the doors open.

This time, Jaxon entered the foyer barking but then quickly turned back to enter the social room. As he did so, he ducked low as if being chased and then, right before my eyes, his hind-end fell to the floor as if spanked or kicked. Simultaneously he yelped and dashed toward us. He would not go back to the foyer until much later.

One has to wonder what it was that scared him so bad.

Perhaps it was the same spirit that replicated this incident in the parsonage in 2004. Or maybe it was the same spirit that in November 2001 came close to making a believer out of a church worker who, I think, prior to this time, doubted the ghostly presence.

One evening, as she was dusting the backs of the pews in the sanctuary, someone or something seemed to grab the dust cloth from her hand and drop it. The incident was a little strange and even more unnerving when, after she had retrieved it and begun to dust again, the cloth was once more pulled away as if by some unseen presence.

It was the first night that she was cleaning alone in the sanctuary.

Maybe the church ghost sought to remind her that she would never be alone, or perhaps it was upset because she wasn't making music.

A short time later, one member of the congregation, a photographer, had volunteered to take family portraits as a fundraiser for the church. It was late in the evening as she sat in the social room waiting for her next appointment to arrive. Amid the normal quiet sounds of the church at night, one sound in particular struck her as rather odd—music. The playing of the pipe organ wafted down from the sanctuary for an extended period of time, yet no one else was in the building. Of the music she recalls, there was only one tune that she recognized—"O Holy Night."

Talking with some members of the congregation after this experience, I learned that one of the former organists of the church, now at rest, had shared an affinity for that hymn. In fact, it was one of her favorites.

There is also a recent tale told that reminds me that, like the other spirits on the properties of St. John, the church ghost may be a bit mischievous.

One spring evening in 2004, two members of the church were working on a carpentry project in the nursery area of the building— preparing a heavy door for the church boiler room by painting it and its hardware. On this day they had moved the door into the church kitchen to utilize its island and make the work easier for them.

As I heard the story, they had painted the door and removed the hardware and had decided to go and get some dinner while the paint dried. They placed all the hardware on the kitchen island and left the building.

When they returned some time later, everything seemed to be as they had left it. But they noted one curious exception. A black handle, which they swore had been placed on the island, appeared to be missing!

Thinking that perhaps they had simply misplaced it, both of the men looked around and retraced their steps. The handle was nowhere to be found.

Finally, one of the men sat down on a bench outside the kitchen area and scratched his head. There, under the island, he saw the black handle.

It was as if something had placed it there to keep it out of sight.

Was it a ghost? Who can really say for sure?

Alarming Office Behavior!

Perhaps no tale of haunting is as sober as that of the Cyrus Stover house. The structure was built in 1858 by the then 28-year-old Stover as a residence for him and his beloved wife, Anna Bunstein. Cyrus was the brother of John L. Riegel's second and third wives, and he worked as a merchant in the post office/general store of the town. He was also an original partner with John L. Riegel in the area's first paper mill.

The story goes that after having built this home and having lived in it for only a brief period of time, Cyrus went off to fight in the Civil War in 1864, serving with the Grand Army of the Republic. Tragically, he died on October 29th of that year during the battle of Athens, Tennessee, perhaps from injuries sustained in combat. The epitaph on his grave in the Riegelsville Union Cemetery reads, "His sun set while it was still noon...."

Even more tragic than his untimely death is the fact that he lies for eternity alone; with his widow not buried at his side. Perhaps it is loneliness, or the tragic nature of his death, but for some reason this Cyrus doesn't seem to lie still. Many believe his ghost wanders the building he was never fully able to live in, and possibly shares the haunt with Mary Louise Aughinbaugh or another spirit. Whatever the case, if the presence in the Stover house is that of Cyrus, he does not seem well adjusted to the present day use of the structure.

My experiences and knowledge of the Stover ghost began in the fall of 1996.

Fig 5. The Cyrus Stover House; built in 1858.

One weekday evening, as a rainstorm was kicking up fog in this small town, I arrived at my office in the Stover house to meet a young couple that was planning to be married. The pastor's office is located on the first floor of this yellow clapboard building—a structure listed on the registry of national historic landmarks. The office is quite elaborate, with floor to ceiling bookshelves and a desk that sits facing into the center of the house. To the left of the desk is a window that looks out at the exterior door of the office that is used to enter the reception area. Through the doorway to the study, one has a view of the foyer at the bottom of the staircase to the second floor.

On this particular evening, I sat with the young couple and listened to their joys and dreams as the rain created echoes on the slate roof two floors above our heads. A cool evening breeze blew through the space around the air conditioner in the porch window and brought a light chill into the room. After about an hour of conversation, I said good night and walked the young couple to the door, returning to my office to finish up some paperwork before I had to leave for a late evening visit with a church family.

Fig 6. Cyrus Stover's Grave in the Union Cemetery, Riegelsville, PA.

The Stover house is very silent when one is there alone. In fact, some have described that silence as smothering. To my amazement, as I sat writing, I heard the screen door of the reception area open, and I heard footsteps come into the building and toward the hall. Slightly alarmed and not expecting anyone, I looked out the window to find the door closed. Peering harder, I couldn't see anyone outside, so I got up from my desk and gingerly made my way out into the hall and back toward the reception area. I remember my heart was pounding as I moved through the doorway and was startled to find the room empty. I checked the screen door one more time to be sure it was latched then hurried back to my desk to finish my work.

No sooner had I sat down, when I was startled by the blaring alarm of an old clock radio on a desk of the reception space, screaming out a mix of music, buzzer, and static! It was so loud that I got up and ran down the hall to shut it off. I now suspected a prankster had come in and began to look around the room and in the old kitchen of the house, but saw no one. I played with the alarm clock and couldn't get the alarm to work again. Frightened, I quickly gathered my things and left for the night.

The next morning I shared my experience of the alarm clock with its owner. To my surprise I learned that the alarm didn't work and hadn't for some time now. The alarm clock disappeared soon after and that was the end of that. Or was it?

Some years later, the office was reconfigured and a new LCD type alarm clock was placed on the same desk in almost the exact spot that the former alarm clock had rested upon. Several times through the following spring, I entered the office to find the alarm blaring away. Each time I would physically have to switch it off. It didn't seem to matter whether I was alone or with other people. I assumed perhaps that it was set as a reminder for someone and that person had simply forgotten to turn it off before they left. But you know what happens when one assumes....

Finally in late May, my curiosity was piqued and I asked about the alarm clock's setting. To my surprise, I learned that it too had never actually been set and folks had no idea how it got switched to the "on" position. The event was scary when combined with the other experienced noises in the office.

The last incident with that alarm clock actually happened one morning while another person and I were sitting at the church computer. Suddenly the alarm clicked on even though it was not set to do so!

It's an interesting phenomena and all too familiar, reminding me of our own bedroom alarm clock that would come on in the middle of the night, or of the clocks that stopped in the early days of my residency in Riegelsville.

The Stover house stories do not stop there however. The other tales are equally as hair-raising.

One person would tell of footsteps and noises that were regularly heard, but were out of the ordinary house sounds, originating on the second floor and in the basement. They would also talk of cats that could be seen wandering the halls, an experience that I have frequently shared while working at my desk. It happens that one sees the tip of a tail or the top of a cat's back pass by at baseboard level out of peripheral vision, but sees nothing when looking fully in that direction. I'm told the former tenant enjoyed having many cats in the house, and allegedly some were found dead in the basement when it was cleaned out upon the tenant's death.

Are these phantom cats one of the former occupant's many pets, some of which were buried on the property or never buried at all?

Another particularly amusing story is that of a Building and Grounds committee meeting held in the large conference room on the first floor of the Stover house.

As the men of the church began their conversations about building maintenance, they very distinctly heard the door to the reception area open, followed by the sound of footsteps crossing that area and coming down the hall toward the meeting room. One of the more curious gentleman, who was always interested in the ghostly property tales, got up to go and meet the latecomer and was startled when nobody was there. The look on his face as he returned to the meeting was classic— it was almost as if he had seen a ghost! It was almost as classic as the looks on the faces of several other men as they realized what it was that they had heard.

The incident prompted my telling of several of the tales I shared when I wrote about the remodeling experiences the church members had encountered at the parsonage several years before.

But if all the tales were so benign, the house would be a fun place to look for ghosts. Such is not the case.

One night in spring 1999, I was in the meeting room downstairs and lost in my thoughts while making copies for a Bible study to be held about fifteen minutes later. As the copier did its work, and my mind daydreamed, I slowly became aware of the lights dimming each time the laser scanned the image. I then noticed out of the corner of my eye something moving. Turning to face the door, I saw a figure rushing toward me with its hand out at stomach level. It was white and fuzzy such that I could not make out details, but I screamed and the image vanished just as a church member opened the door to arrive for Bible study. She found me alarmed and white-faced.

Then in 2001, a previous pastor told one chillingly similar tale of being at that copier, in the same room, in spring 1994. It was about 8:30 P.M. in the evening. As the pastor finished her photocopying, she turned to gather her things and felt as if an unseen presence punched her in the stomach. Though she heard nothing, in her head ran the words, "Get out. Get out now!"

She grabbed at her bags to get them together and rushed to the hallway, only to feel pushed down the hall and toward the door of the secretary's office. As she rushed out the door, her attaché case caught on the door's handle and she turned to wrestle it free as the presence slammed the door in her face. Quickly moving to her car, the presence seemed to follow her until she was part way out of town.

I believe that "Cyrus" may be curious or perhaps a little fearful of the present equipment stored in his home, or of the current use of the building. One visitor on the Riegelsville Public Library's Haunted Walking Tours of 2001 claimed to be sensitive to supernatural energy. As her tour guide stood telling the ghostly tales before the Stover house, she claimed to have felt a connection with the spirit of Cyrus Stover who still lived in the house. She relates that he didn't understand what the copy machine was and why it was in his home.

Perhaps "Cyrus" doesn't understand the change in times and is lost in the world of the 1860s without electronic equipment. Perhaps he doesn't *like* the change in times. Nevertheless, the electronic equipment in the church office seems to be a focal point around which there is some supernatural activity.

In fact, one person tells the story of walking into the copy room and meeting area of the office where, at the time, several unused computer parts were kept. Coming through the door and walking to the copier on the far side of the room, this person was surprised to see one of the computer keyboards flip itself off the table where it rested, half on and half off, as if it had been hit like on a springboard.

There is also another story told from the Stover home that is related to electronic equipment. Many ghost hunters tell of supernatural phenomena creating havoc with electrical equipment such as cameras or audio and video recorders. In late fall 1998, or spring 1999, three church members and I sat down in my office one evening to read lines for a play that we were planning to perform later that year. Our night was to consist of reading through the script and recording the session so that we could practice our lines by listening to the tape. The recorders that we used had worked fine in other settings, just within hours of this experience.

It was around 7:00 P.M. when we started the first of the three taping sessions. During our time together there was a strange feeling in the house and I think we may have even heard the reception area door open and close again, but otherwise the night went off without a hitch. Or so we thought.

Several days later one of the three called another to see if she could borrow the other's recording of the night's sessions, because the one she had made seemed to have nothing on it. The other member replied that her tape didn't come out either. The third member had the same problem and, I must say—my tape didn't come out right either. The recordings were overwhelmed by a static that made it hard to discern our voices even though the microphones had been sitting less than two feet from our mouths!

The experiences continued. In May 1999, another story was told of a ghostly encounter in the office in the middle of the afternoon. This individual experienced the door to the receptionist's room slowly push open, allowing a cold breeze to enter from the hallway. Uncomfortable, she got up from what she was doing and went into the old kitchen of the house, recently converted to a copy room, only to feel the breeze enter with her. A warm hand then touched her shoulder, upon which she jumped and moved back into the receptionist's area. In moments, the cold breeze moved back through the room into the hallway and pulled the door closed behind it. She quickly finished up for the day and went home. This same person also would hear strange noises on the second floor and took to closing the door that separated the reception area from the rest of the house.

One day in May 2000, the Stover house experiences grew even more interesting.

It is important to remember that this is the place where, in 1867, Mary Louise Aughinbaugh died in one of the upstairs rooms from tuberculosis. Some say she still walks its floors. Others surmise that perhaps Marion Riegel haunts here because she lived in the home a short time while her own dwelling was under construction. No one can say for certain whose spirit accompanies Cyrus on his haunts, but on this afternoon, there was definitely a female presence in the house.

It was a warm day as a church volunteer sat again in the reception area. As she tells it, it was quiet in the building. At some point through the afternoon, she became aware of a noise on the steps to the second floor and of the fact that she hadn't closed the hallway door today. Glancing down the hall to see what was going on, there she beheld the white ghostly image of a woman walking down the stairs and crossing into the meeting room—the room that formerly held the copier. She says she then heard noises in that room as if things were being moved around. In a short time, the image came back through the hall and floated back up the stairs again. After that day, the door to the rest of the home was always closed while she worked there!

No matter if one spirit or two, the Stover home is definitely not a place I would wish to spend the night! This was a fact emphasized for me during one of the Haunted Walking Tours of 2002.

It was a cold and rainy Friday night and we had offered a midnight tour of the town's ghostly areas. My wife and I were the tour guides and we had spaced out the trip so that we wouldn't run into each other's group along our way through town.

Shortly after midnight, I took a small group of young men and women into the Stover house to tell its ghostly tales. Slowly we walked along the shadowy hallway downstairs toward the conference room. There we settled in for some spirited storytelling. I had just finished sharing the sad fate of Cyrus Stover and Mary Louisa Aughinbaugh when, very clearly, heavy footsteps walked across the ceiling of the downstairs meeting room! Obviously, something was moving around on the second floor.

The sound was so startling that I stopped my tale in mid-sentence and grew quiet. The group before me laughed at first but then, seeing how quiet I had gotten and the obvious shock on my face, they grew very rattled.

"That's part of the tour," one of them said with bravado and half jokingly.

Another added, "Isn't it?"

I said, "No. But then again, it is a ghost tour, and who can predict what will happen."

They were eager to get out of the building.

I am sure that the fresh rain that night never felt so good as when they got outside and left behind whatever it was that was walking about on the Stover home's historic floors!

Opening Doors

In December 1999 and January 2000, my wife and I were reminded once again that we shared our home with some entity that we could not explain.

Around the time the church suffered its string of stripped light switches, we found that we could not keep the doors closed that separated our bedroom from the rest of the house.

It was late in the night and my wife and I were sleeping soundly under some heavy blankets, protected from the late night chills. Or so we thought.

We rested peacefully, having insulated ourselves from the rest of the house by closing two doors between our bedroom and the second floor hallway. Not a sound could be heard. Then, from a deep sleep, I heard the door to our room creak open accompanied by the ringing of a little Japanese bell hanging from its doorknob. I turned my head and looked up in time to see the door swing to a full open position, but no one was there and there was no logical explanation for what had caused the movement.

In the past, curious cats have pushed open doors in the house that were not tightly closed but, when they would do this, they would then enter the rooms. On the occasions when they would enter our bedroom, within seconds of the door opening, one or more cats would then spring up onto the bed to snuggle with us.

This night I waited, but no cat jumped up to announce its presence and the only sound to be heard after the creaking and the ringing stopped, was silence.

Slowly, I got out of bed and saw that the door to the hall was also open. Now my curiosity was piqued. I left the room to look around and carefully found my way into the second floor hall. A few seconds later my wife came out and told me that she had seen a shadow moving in the middle bedroom. Still not seeing anything to explain the doors or the shadow, we eventually went back to bed—tightly closing the doors behind us.

For the next several nights, before going to sleep I would slam the doors closed and pull on the knobs to make sure that they simply couldn't pop open with a push. Despite my best efforts however, on at least two more occasions, the doors opened. Finally, after several nights of restless sleep and on the last night of the string of events, as our creaking bedroom door swung open, the clock radio across the room began to blare music. It was 3 A.M. The alarm was set for six o'clock!

Each time the doors opened, the cats could be found asleep in the hall.

Then, as strangely as the phenomena started, it stopped.

But the ghostly affinity with doors doesn't seem to have ended there.

Early in June 2000, we were preparing to go out one evening, and I took our male cat and his mother and put them in an upstairs bedroom to give them privacy and keep them safe. We had adopted these two cats in 1998, and they had never quite adjusted to the others. In order to keep all the cats happy, Poohbelle and Delice had their own room where they would sleep at night and spend time while we were away.

On this particular night they would have been in the room for several hours and seemed content. I opened the door to their room and said goodbye, smiling at Poohbelle's funny face and at Delice, who was playing bedpost. This was the term my wife and I had coined for the times when she would hide under the bed by sitting with her body along the leg of the headboard and tucking her head up near the mattress as if no one could see her! Knowing they were safe, I closed the door and descended to the first floor to begin gathering the things we needed for our evening out.

Only a few moments had passed when I heard my wife opening doors and calling for Pooh. I went to the staircase and told her he was locked in the bedroom. She replied that she couldn't find him.

Finally, I heard her exclaim, "What were you doing in there?" He had been found sitting inside the door to the third floor staircase, crying to get out.

There are also other tales of opening doors in the parsonage, some of which come with a bit of a twist, such as one from a more recent experience in the early spring of 2004.

My wife was home alone late one Sunday evening after I had gone to the church to teach a confirmation class. She moved about upstairs getting ready to leave to meet her family for dinner and, in the process, periodically worked at moving laundry from the washer to the dryer.

On one instance when she was in the laundry room, she was startled when, right before her eyes, the door to the dryer opened all the way by itself, as if someone was checking to see if the clothes were dry. Even more curious was the fact that the motor continued running! Within seconds the door closed again.

She went over to it and opened the door. The motor stopped running.

In the course of the next several days, on multiple occasions, the dryer door opened while it was running and either my wife or I noticed the activity.

As with the other strings of incidents, one day it suddenly stopped.

In almost every case, whether they are stories of doors opening or of seeing strange things, the ghostly tales in our house are startling. Yet one evening's activity is a good example of the times when our haunting seems to reach a level of creating uneasiness that isn't easily communicated with words.

It was a Wednesday night and I waited for my wife to arrive home from work by lying down in our bedroom and eagerly trying to finish the book that I had been reading. I suddenly grew thirsty. My muscles sore, I stretched out a bit and set my book down on a table near the bed. I looked out the window and noticed that evening was settling in and the shadows were getting longer as the sun set for the night.

Slowly, I took my time moving around and eventually found my way downstairs to the kitchen and proceeded to quench my thirst with a much-needed glass of water. The thought then occurred to me to check the weather and flip some channels on the television, so I moved into the living room to indulge myself. Crossing through that room, my eyes were drawn to the coffee table and I am sure I even blinked! There, lying neatly on the table was the book I had been reading upstairs—even marked to the page where I had left it!

Now this was a little troubling, but I managed to see some humor in the episode until I sat down to finish reading and, out of the corner of my eye, saw a cat sitting in the center of the floor. It looked like Nightshade so I called out and looked up only to discover that the image was gone. Baffled, I ventured around the house and found her sound asleep, snuggled on my desk in the office, apparently not having moved in quite a while. Now my nerves were beginning to be irritated and I grew frightened.

Trying to calm down, I sat and took some deep breaths when, to my delight, I heard Stephanie's car alarm beep on, indicating that she had arrived home from work. Jumping up, I hurried down the hall to greet her, only to find that her car wasn't in the driveway and there was no sign of her presence.

By the time she finally did arrive home, I was sitting on the porch—just happy to have a familiar face around and to feel the comfort of no longer being alone with whatever it is that periodically manifests itself in our house.

Ghost Tours and Detection

A new dimension to our experience of the ghosts in Riegelsville began in October 2000. That fall, my wife and I agreed to help coordinate the Riegelsville Public Library's Haunted Walking Tours. In fact, we volunteered to be two of several guides on the tours in the hopes of sharing our stories and experiences, and of hearing the tales of others in town.

The venture began on a Friday, the thirteenth of October. That night, we gathered with family and friends in the cold light of a full moon, and shared in a preview tour of the neighborhood. It was decided that, even with the bright moon's glow, we would ask those homes along our route to turn on as many outside lights as possible to help people navigate along the sidewalks. Stephanie and I turned on several lights in and around our house.

The tour was successful and without incident.

After its conclusion, we debriefed with some folks in the parking lot of the borough building and then walked back to our house. Crossing the porch from the driveway, Stephanie and I talked about the tours we had just shared and offered suggestions to each other for making them better, then unlocked the door and stepped inside. Immediately, we were aware that something was different.

About 3 feet inside the kitchen door, a gold metal decorative bracket rested, oddly out of place and not immediately recognizable. We looked at each other in curiosity and began to scour the kitchen to see if we could determine the bracket's source. A few minutes later, it became obvious that the bracket had come off of a light that hangs in the entranceway of the house—held in place by a screw. The screw was now missing and the bracket had fallen a good five feet away from where it should have fallen in the area under the light.

Later that month, I volunteered to take a group from *Prevention* magazine on a private Friday afternoon tour and gathered with them to share our stories. A few hours later, I returned home to find that the doors to the upstairs bedrooms, standing wide open when I had left, had all now been closed by some unseen presence.

But this phantom playfulness wasn't the only thing that got our attention during the period in which we shared these ghost walks. In fact, it chilled us less than the stories told to my wife and me by town residents who walked with us about the neighborhood. These were far more interesting, and disturbing.

One such tale shared by a former town inhabitant is that of his experience in our home while visiting in an upstairs room with a former pastor's son. As he tells the story, they sat playing in the room and were startled when a man, dressed in the uniform of a Revolutionary War soldier, stepped through the wall beside them and looked at the boys inquisitively, then vanished.

An equally disturbing tale was shared with us by a youth whose mother used to clean for one of the former pastors. She tells of cleaning in a middle room on the second floor of the house, and being startled occasionally by the image of a black cat that appeared in different parts of the room. This is the same room that also seemed to hold a very unsettling feeling in it on the instances when the doors to our bedroom would open late at night.

There is no doubt that our home has a history of haunting—visual and, as we were soon to be aware, quantifiable.

On February 4, 2001, my brother came to visit and brought with him an electromagnetic frequency detector he had bought online. Ghost hunters use this device to detect the presence of a magnetic field that is often associated with spiritual activity. That day, he and I walked through the entire downstairs of the house, only to find that the detector had no reaction unless held within two feet of the computer monitor in my office. It activated the unit's sensors and sent its lights to the highest readings.

Satisfied now that we knew the two-foot range of detection, my brother and I traveled up the stairs from the first floor, unit in hand, and walked through the second floor without incident. Then we went on up to the third floor.

We had walked through all the rooms, again without incident, when I remembered we hadn't entered the cubby space in the room where most others had felt supernatural energy. Opening that door, I stepped in with the unit held before me in an outstretched hand. Gently moving it back and forth, I smiled as nothing happened, yet inside felt disappointment. Then as I turned to leave, in the corner of the cubby, the sensor suddenly was activated and it lit up with brilliant red lights—reading at its highest levels! The lights stayed on for a second or two then disappeared. Within moments, the red lights went back on again for a short time then darkened. No matter where the sensor was moved within that cubby space, its lights did not come back on. Digital pictures taken during this time showed nothing except an empty room.

As we closed the cubby door and turned back into our living space however, once more we were greeted by red lights on the unit. Swiftly, they darkened for a third time. The unit's sensors were activated one more time outside the door of that room and then nothing more could be found.

A little nervous and excited, we went downstairs and discovered that, on the main staircase from the first floor, the sensor was tripped once more. This time the lights indicated another full reading! In addition, the entire center section of the staircase was filled with this spirit-presence and pockets of cold air that could be felt in addition to seeing the readings on this EMD unit. My wife joined us at this point.

"Talk to it," my brother said.

"If you can understand me," I started, "then step off the stairs and move away from me."

Within a second, the red lights on the detector slowly decreased and then turned dark.

"Come back," I called.

Within seconds the red lights began to slowly come on again.

"Go to the top of the stairs," I instructed.

When we went to the top of the stairs to see if it had obeyed us, the detector could find nothing.

Amazed at the experience we just shared, our excited conversation filled the silence in the house. Suddenly, I had a realization and ran to the second floor, heading toward a back and little-used staircase that runs from our kitchen to the second floor laundry area. It was only a whim, but a good one I soon learned. Opening the door at the top of these stairs, we were amazed when slowly the red lights started to increase again! The presence had obeyed, but in its own playful way, having gone to the top of another staircase in a phantom game of hide and seek. Moments later, the lights grew dark again and the presence didn't return that day.

A week later, I took the detector in hand downstairs and turned it on. Moving about, its lights remained dark. However, I was startled when, having turned quickly to retrace my steps, the lights flashed on and detected a presence behind me. They quickly went dark again!

A third event happened on the evening of March 3, 2001, as a blizzard approached the area. That night, I went to the third floor to get some flashlight batteries out of our camping gear and took the detector along on a whim, turning it on and setting it down in the center of the room. As I gathered the batteries, out of the corner of my eye, I noticed that the red lights were slowly creeping on. I reached out and grabbed the device and spoke to the empty room.

"Hello?"

The red lights increased to a full detection. I managed to walk with the essence back toward that same storage space where the lights had first detected something weeks before. There, the red lights dimmed and the presence vanished. Nothing was found inside. I turned and, as before, closed the door to the cubby space, moving back into our living area. The red lights rapidly lit up again! Finally, the detector sensed another hit in the hallway on the third floor. After that nothing more happened.

For me, this unit has confirmed what I already knew. There is a presence that seems to reside on the third floor of our home and it often seeks company with those who live and breathe within the parsonage walls.

A Treasury of Tales

Summer 2001 seemed to offer a respite to any ghostly activity in our home as days and weeks went by without incident. Then in late August, we had another ghostly reminder that we were not alone.

On this occasion, my brother had come to spend the night as a stopover point on the way to his work site of the next day. The hours together offered us a chance to visit and catch up. Most of the evening was uneventful except for a few moments when, during a walk in the cemetery, we visited Louisa's grave. There my brother was pretty insistent in asking her to behave that night and leave him alone (as he would be sleeping in the room where so often ghostly phenomena seemed to occur). Before long, we retired for some sleep and my brother went into his room and closed the door.

The next morning as Stephanie and I readied for work, we both commented that the door to his room was open. This was curious, but not at all unusual. The door to that room opens by itself in either day or night and this activity is a regular phenomenon.

When my brother awoke, he told us that in the middle of the night the door to his room had slammed open. Startling him, he rubbed his eyes and saw one cat in the room with him, sleeping on the next bed. Quickly, he stood up and looked out into the hall to find another cat sleeping on a bureau, but far enough away that logic dictated she couldn't have pushed the door open. Nothing else happened and eventually he went back to sleep.

It soon came time for Stephanie to leave for work and, as usual, I walked with her to the same door which we use every day and she unlocked the deadbolt and the latch. Turning the knob, she pulled—but the door wouldn't move. After a few seconds of tugging, I too tried to pull the door open and it wouldn't move for me either. She tried one more time and gave up.

We exited the house through another door and, as her car pulled out of the driveway, I came across the porch as always and turned the same knob that moments before had stubbornly refused to release its door. It easily swung open! I stood in amazement, reflecting that it was as if a ghostly hand had been holding the door closed, only to release it when we decided to give up on its trick. That door had opened many times without a person nearby. This was the first time though, that it had been held closed.

Later that afternoon, another mysterious event occurred. I had been out sharing in some pastoral visits and had come home for a brief stop before heading to the church office. Turning that same doorknob, I entered the house and laughed to myself that the door had once again opened so easily. The house was quiet. I walked the hall to the main staircase of the house and started up to the second floor. About halfway through the climb, water dripped down on my head from some unseen source. I looked up and saw nothing to explain the trickling flow, yet still I had been doused with enough water to wet my hair and face. The ceiling was bone dry.

The following October brought two of the most curious incidents yet.

October 19, 2001, marked an opportunity for us to have friends over in order to say goodbye to a colleague who was leaving the area. As the evening moved along, around 10:30 P.M., another clergy couple sat with my wife and me in our sitting room, listening as we told them ghost stories in order to ease their curiosity. I mentioned the detector my brother had given us and told a few of the stories about its use on the staircase and in some of our upstairs rooms. The wife of this couple asked to see how it worked. Now, I had demonstrated the detector before so, thinking nothing of it, I turned the device on and walked over to the television to show the magnetic field and the red lights it created on the unit.

As I did so, my wife commented that we often do not talk about the ghost because when we do, it seems to show up. Everybody laughed and we made some random comment about how interesting that would be. I clicked off the television and turned back toward the center of the room. Suddenly, the red lights of the unit turned on until it read a full presence. Our curious guest then took the detector in hand and turned to scan the room. The lights dimmed. Then, just as she turned back toward us, the lights came on right in the middle of where we were all standing. They held briefly and then went out. As in previous gatherings in our home, the ghost seemed to come and visit our party.

The second incident happened the following Monday. Once again it was time to prepare for the library's Haunted Walking Tours and the tour guides had gathered at our house to refresh themselves on the many stories in town that we would be sharing with our curious guests. Partway into the discussion, again the topic of the detector came up and I took it out to show the other guides. We walked around in anticipation with the unit in hand, but nothing ghostly seemed to be about on the first floor. Laughing, they went back into the living room and into their conversation, but I ascended the staircase to the second floor only to find that right at the top of the stairs the red lights of the unit came on.

On the fourth of July, my father and I had the exact same experience as the detector went off at the top of the stairs and at the bottom of the third floor steps, at a height just above the hardwood floor. The red lights darkened again. I called to the other guides to come upstairs and everyone but my wife came up. As they arrived at the top of the steps, I was able to use the detector and follow the presence down the hallway toward the third floor staircase. Outside the door to those stairs, a pocket of cold air seemed to dance and hover. Each of the five of us placed a hand in the pocket of cold air and tried to follow it as it floated about in space.

Then, in an incredible moment, one of the guides tested the cold pocket by trying to determine its parameters using the palm of her hand. As we each began to follow suit, it became readily apparent that the cold pocket was spherical in shape! This immediately reminded me of floating orbs, which have been described in many a book as indicating the presence of a supernatural entity. Here we were with our own orb, floating and allowing us to "hold" it. After a few moments the cold pocket disappeared and only later briefly reappeared at the top of the staircase to the first floor.

In early November, I shared this tale with a member of the church who commented that she too had experienced a ghostly encounter in this part of the parsonage. This woman shared with me that, during the tenure of my predecessor, she had stayed with the pastor for a weekend while visiting family and had slept in a second floor bedroom at the bottom of the stairs to the third floor.

One night, while the pastor was away, she lay down to sleep and after a while was startled by the sound of footsteps coming toward her room. There was supposedly nobody home! Closer they came until the door to her room swung open and a woman dressed in old-fashioned clothing stepped across the threshold. The apparition didn't seem to notice its live cohabitant. Instead, it turned and looked out a window toward the highway and the river beyond. Unable to speak, this church member watched until the figure soon disappeared!

For almost a year, the house was quiet again. Then in 2002, again in the fall, we had another round of activity.

In late September, my brother and his fiancé and I toured the church properties with a heat-sensor, electromagnetic field detector, digital camera, and video camera. In all three properties we discovered milky white orbs present on the videotape footage—orbs that could not be seen with the naked eye. They appeared to be floating and emanating light. Many claim these orbs are the souls of people who have passed on; that they are evidence of the spirit's energy.

If I had not been there to see with my naked eye the empty rooms, in contrast to the video and digital pictures, I myself may not have believed what we found.

Fig 7. Orbs in the sanctuary: St. John UCC.

One orb in particular, in the sanctuary, rose up off a pew about 8 feet and then moved at a right angle toward the windows—rapidly passing through the wall and disappearing into the night. Others could be seen concentrated in the balcony and choir loft areas of the building. Curiously, these are areas where folks have felt or seen a spectral presence.

Similarly, in the Stover house, orbs appeared on the pictures exposed in the first floor meeting room, at the foot of the staircase, and in the rooms of the third floor above. One orb on the third floor, in particular, was unsettling. It appeared as a deep red in color. I've tried to find others who have seen a similar orb and haven't been able to locate anyone. My theory is that perhaps the red color indicates an angry spirit. I would suppose this could be the spirit of Cyrus Stover— based on some of the unsettling things that have been experienced in the Stover home.

The red orb appeared in another photo as well, but lighter in color. Curiously, when the second photo was taken, I was mentally trying to assure Cyrus we meant him no harm. The orb appeared right above my shoulder.

The season's haunting continued the week of October 13, when psychic activity picked up in our home as well. On several occasions, my wife related that she felt that something had been present in different areas of the house. In particular, she told the story of lying in bed one evening and hearing an object bounce on the ceiling, as if dropped on the third floor above her. It sounded like wood or metal, but the room from where the sound emerged had been empty for years.

Later that week, a funny, yet memorable experience occurred. My wife was sitting alone at the counter in the first floor kitchen and working on her laptop. I sat two rooms away at our home computer writing a sermon. For a period of time we both stayed in these places and busily labored until we needed a break.

It was just at one of those moments when, while stretching muscles and waiting for her computer to do its thing, my wife reports that she tapped the stylus of her laptop on the counter in a rhythm, not really thinking anything of it.

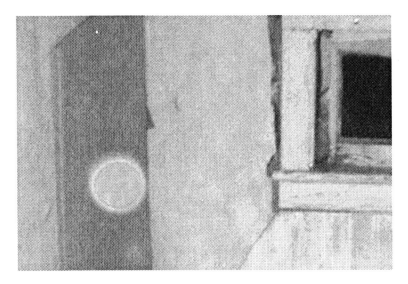

Fig 8. A red orb in the Stover house: sign of an angry spirit?

Suddenly, she was surprised to hear the sound of something tapping a dish to the same rhythm in one of the cabinets across the room. Curious, she tapped the stylus consciously this time, in a specific pattern, and waited. Not too long passed before the rhythm played back on the dish again.

A gasp of surprise was all she could manage, startling me as I sat two rooms away!

One thing is certain. As the years go by, through periods of psychic activity and silence, we are certain that in the three buildings of the church properties, we are not alone.

It's as if a spectral energy moves back and forth among the buildings on this hill of the town, watching, looking after, and sometimes causing some mischief toward those who live and work within them!

Perhaps this lends credibility to the person who, during our walking tours of 2001, claimed sensitivity to an energy field in the space between the parsonage and the main building of the John S. Riegel estate— another structure built by the Riegel family and sitting on this hill!

101

The John S. Riegel Estate

The main route through Riegelsville was, at one time, a dirt street that was well worn and traveled by peddlers and many other merchants seeking to make a living as they journeyed along Easton Road between the city of Easton proper and Philadelphia.

Peering back through the sands of time, one cannot help but imagine those days when the horse drawn wagons would slowly roll their way along, stopping at the properties they passed in order to sell their wares in this scenic, sleepy village. No doubt, many of the present day homes could tell the tale of watching the exchange of goods for money, followed by the distinct dust clouds that would rise behind the small peddlers' wagons as they completed a sale and moved along to their next opportunity. It was another time in this town's history, when the fields were more abundant and the property lines were less distinct and seemed to flow, rather than be separated by the modern rigidity of concrete roads and wire fencing.

One such tract of land that has truly felt the onset of modern property division is that of the John S. Riegel estate. Originally flowing down over the hill and sweeping across the peddlers' road and the pasture beyond, this property extended from the Delaware Canal west to the modern day St. Lawrence Roman Catholic Church.

While the view and the fields were beautiful to behold, the most striking sight on the Riegel property was, and yet remains, the main house that stands at the crest of a hill overlooking the paved and very modern Route 611 and the grassy fields beyond.

Fig 9. From Left to Right: St. John UCC, The Stover House, The Academy Building, St. John Parsonage, and the John S. Riegel Estate. Ca. 1900 (Courtesy of Ann Anderson).

Constructed between 1892 and 1896, this stone structure in the Queen Anne and Tudor style boasts a vast living area and spacious grounds. Kathleen Cook writes, "according to Riegel family tradition, the house was designed by Marion Griffin Riegel, who studied architecture at Cornell University before marrying John Stover Riegel" (Cook 132). According to the history I was told, Marion was one of the earliest female graduates from Cornell and, upon her graduation, John offered to build the house of Marion's dreams.

John S. Riegel was the son of John L. Riegel and his third wife, Lydia Stover. John attended the Riegelsville Academy in town and graduated with a degree in engineering from Lehigh University in 1890. While their home was being built, John and Marion lived in the Cyrus Stover house.

The Greystone Manor, as it is called today, may have been the only architectural project Marion ever designed and completed. In December 1895, the family prepared to move in, along with a governess, and in the rear of the property lived the coachman, James Murphy, and his family.

In 1896, just as construction was ending on the house, a rogue lightning bolt struck the north side of the building and caused enough damage that the wall needed to be razed and reconstructed. Later that same year, the Riegels settled in their new home.

In 1899, John Riegel was promoted to General Manager of the family's paper mill and expanded the family business. He created a jute rope factory to aid in packaging for the paper mill and moved his family to New York, settling in Brooklyn. Their Riegelsville home was then used on weekends and for family vacations.

Marion Riegel died of typhoid fever in 1905, at the young age of 33, and John sold the estate in 1916 (Cook 133).

The next owners subdivided the property, and the former carriage house became a private dwelling. In the middle to late 1900s, the main home continued in its function as a private residence to a couple and their children. This family shared a joyous time on the vast grounds and in the many rooms of the house until the home was sold again in the mid 1980s (Cook 134).

Two of the children from this family relate that, during the time they lived there, some unexplainable phenomena occurred within the home. One child tells the story that a woman's ghost would walk about on the third floor, though the family's mother always said there was no such thing. Another recalled sleeping in their room on the second floor. This child said that they would sometimes tell their mother that they couldn't sleep at night because, "the ghost kept coming down the stairs from the third floor, floating down the hall to [their] room." As an adult, this child shared that even though they couldn't explain it, they are sure there was a ghost of a woman in that home.

In the 1980s, the main house became known as the Greystone Manor and functioned as a bed and breakfast for a brief period of time, after which it returned to use as a private residence (Cook 133).

Almost 100 years to the date of its construction, the John S. Riegel estate found itself lovingly cared for again by a couple who fell in love with the property and then discovered a deep connection and appreciation of its history—as if it was meant to be theirs.

The wife of this couple was a graduate of the Cornell University School of Architecture, Art, and Planning, as was Marion Riegel. Further, she was 25 when she met her husband, who was 50. It is recorded that Marion Riegel married John when she was 25 and he was 50! Even more remarkable is the fact that the husband of this new couple had owned a building in New York called the Brooklyn Union Gas Factory. In its history, it was a jute rope factory called the Couples Rope Factory, which was previously owned by the Riegel family. The husband had also owned the Riegel home in New York.

He and his new wife found themselves commuting to Riegelsville for weekends, just as in the footsteps of the Riegels a century earlier. Perhaps even more striking in the similarities between this couple and the Riegels is that, in April 1996, a hundred years after that rogue lightning bolt damaged the main house of the estate, the home again sustained a fire. This time, the cause was internal and the building sustained major damage. The owners painstakingly had the house restored to its previous grandeur.

It's almost as if history was repeating itself or the echoes of the past were being played out in the present. The experience of the Riegels seemed to stretch out over time like the ripples a rock creates when it is thrown into a pond. The waves move along and can later be felt by some distant object.

Studies have shown that in many homes where the history of the structure seems to repeat itself, or reconstruction occurs on a grand scale, psychic activity seems to increase—as if the spirits wish to communicate.

Such may be the case on the Riegel estate. For it seems that Marion Riegel may have shared an affinity for a fellow alumnus, and may have desired to live vicariously through the wife of this couple or to get to know her better—hoping perhaps, that this couple could help her house to settle and be secure for a time. Imagine if you will, the pain a spirit would experience in watching its family estate subdivided over time. Perhaps the spirit does not understand and wants to feel and see its property be whole again.

Whatever the explanation, the main house was the site of some unexplainable activity during the period of this couple's residency.

The top floor of the Greystone was originally the servants' quarters, but was converted in the late 1990s into a guest area and bathrooms. During this particular couple's occupancy, one of those bedrooms was used as an office space overlooking Elmwood Lane.

On several occasions while her husband was away, the wife of this couple would be working in this room and hear distinct footsteps walking up and down the hallway behind her. Without explanation, doors to the rooms along that hallway would also open and slam shut. When she went into the area to check on the strange activity, nothing could be seen. She soon learned to ignore it.

On some occasions though, it couldn't be ignored. She relates that sometimes the televisions in the third floor guest rooms would turn off and on in the dead of the night, breaking the silence of the home. But whenever someone would go upstairs to investigate, they would find everything dark and quiet.

There are also tales told by several friends of the couple who visited periodically and began to request that on their visits they only sleep on the 2nd floor. They claimed that something scary was on the third floor, something that made them feel chilled—something dark. The feeling was strongest in one large bedroom at the end of that infamous hallway. This room soon got nicknamed by one of their friends for a rather suicidal poet. He claimed that whenever he stayed there he had dark and suicidal thoughts.

Finally, the wife recalls that on one or two occasions, she would run up the stairs to retrieve something from her office and on those stairs she would detect a chill in the air such that the hair on her arms would stand up.

After the fire in 1996, and the subsequent restoration and sale of the home to more recent owners, it seems the spirit of the home may have stayed active long enough to feel that the house was in good hands yet again.

One of the recent owners described feeling drawn to the house and having a spiritual connection to it that seemed present even on the first visit.

Perhaps the spirit called these owners to live there and then decided to watch over them to make sure everything was fine.

This would seem to be the case, at least as evidenced by the tale one of them tells from an afternoon working in a room on the third floor.

This gentleman was sitting in the same office space as the previous owner when he became aware of a presence behind him that seemed to be walking toward his back. When he turned to look for the unexpected arrival, the only evidence of someone's presence to be found was in hearing the floorboards creak as if someone was walking out of the room and into the hallway beyond.

He was not the only one to feel that something else was in the house. Another resident recalls an awareness of something unusual as they watched television one evening. He saw a shadow moving along the wall that seemed to be that of a person. No one present was in a place to cause it.

Still another experience has been shared that happened one day as the owners were exercising in a basement room. As they were working out there, the image of a woman, whom they did not recognize, passed the doorway and looked in on them before moving away.

Within a short time, the sightings ended. Yet some of the women, who have periodically worked on the third floor of the house, seem to describe feeling a presence with them that seems to watch over them. They have nicknamed this entity, "the governess."

Yet it seems that for all the unusual activity within its walls, the alleged spirit of the home, perhaps the spirit of Marion Riegel, is now content.

When you think about it, it's not really that hard to understand why the desire to feel content or whole again would be important for a spirit. Some call death the final healing and depict the life after this mortal one as one of complete wholeness—where our souls no longer endure the pain and suffering of this existence, but feel free and complete.

The desire to share this feeling of wholeness or healing with those still in the mortal world perhaps motivates those spirits who have passed on to relate to us who are left behind. At least this would seem to be the case for those residing in the carriage house of the Riegel estate.

Residents there tell the story that, one year, the children in the home received the gift of some mugs shaped like Easter Bunnies. These were special mugs because when you poured liquid in them, depending on the temperature, they would play a melody. They were used for a period of time and then, like most childhood gifts, were placed in a cabinet or on a shelf and rarely touched. For ten years the mugs sat unused and it was thought that perhaps they may not have even have worked any longer.

Soon, the father of the family took sick.

As it was told to me, the story goes that in the times when the father's illness seemed the worst, the mugs would begin playing their melody. This happened as often as three times a week.

Some time later, the wife of the house was hospitalized with a life-threatening illness. She relates that, upon returning home and during her recovery, as she moved about through the house, she would see a shadow following her around. It was there whether she traveled up the stairs, through the rooms, or anywhere she went. Now, to be clear, she relates that during the times this shadow was observed, the house was dark and there was no sun. Yet still one could see this mysterious shadow.

The woman's daughter allegedly consulted a psychic, who said that the presence was that of the woman's spirit, seeking to make her whole again! Perhaps that could account for the disembodied footsteps heard travelling in the house at times.

Another explanation though, could be that those footsteps belong to someone else seeking to care for the family. They could belong to the ghost of a woman whom the children of the home recall seeing through a window of the other half of the house one day. She was baking bread in an old wood stove. Who knows?

As the sands of time shift and change, and the world around us moves farther away from the sights and sounds of the past, one thing seems constant. The desire for the human spirit to be at peace and feel whole seems to stretch across the boundaries of life and death!

The changes over time on the John S. Riegel estate may explain the psychic activity on its grounds. Then again, there could be another reason for this activity; one that is darkened to the human mind—one that only the spirits know.

The Riegelsville Academy Building

I recently came across an old photo of children from the Riegelsville Academy who were posed, along with their schoolmaster, on a lawn in front of the building. Staring into the burnt sienna image, I could almost envision the children moving about full of joy and life.

In fact, standing on the lawn at the rear of the building, I sometimes listen in the silence of the evening to the peals of children's laughter carried on the winds of time from decades past—laughter that was caught up in a breeze as the children ran and played after a day of learning in the classroom.

Another of John L. Riegel's legacies, the Riegelsville Academy Building was constructed in 1885 with the intention of housing a Public Library, the Riegelsville Academy, and a private living quarters for the Academy's principal (Cook 135). The structure was dedicated on September 11, 1886, and managed by the congregation of St. John Reformed Church, now St. John UCC. Its purpose was to be a co-educational preparatory school for the children of the mill workers and, in its time, 370 students attended the building, with 80 graduating.

The decades were kind to the academy in Riegelsville and the building continued in its function as a public library well after the school closed its doors in 1916. Many a town resident, past and present, has walked its floors, daydreamed while looking out its windows, or crossed over its threshold.

In the 1960s, the Public Library closed for a period of years until

109

**Fig 10. The Old Academy Building, which is now the site of the
Riegelsville Public Library and Borough Hall.**

some townspeople began pushing for it to be re-opened. Their efforts
succeeded and the Library's presence in the community was restored in
1976. One can only wonder what happened within its walls in the years
when the bookshelves were untouched.

With so many children having spent long hours within the confines
of the library space, would it be unusual if some of their souls still had
a hunger for learning and were intent on spending time in death among
the books of knowledge they had enjoyed in life? Were there some
children whose lives were tragically ended before they could graduate,
who wander in the halls of learning and wait for that glorious,
unreachable day?

After the Library reopened its doors, several folks in town tell the
story that some unusual activity began to be noticed. I've heard several
accounts of the ghostly happenings from this time period and, while
many differ on details, they are consistent on one fact: the spirit of a
disembodied young girl seemed to be present along the many
bookshelves of the library's one large room. One town resident recalls
being in the library and encountering this entity as it stood among the
book stacks tossing volumes of texts from the shelves to the floor.

Despite the various sources for *this* account of the spirit's presence, one former librarian refutes its details and instead offers the following story as an eyewitness to the ghostly image.

It was a late evening and the Library Board was meeting to conduct its monthly business. As the group worked within these historic walls, a sensation began to build for one woman there, who claimed to be sensitive to psychic activity. She stopped the folks in their work and commented that while they were in conversation, the spirit of a little girl appeared in the kitchen area on the south side of the library. Unfortunately there is no present day description of this spirit's appearance, but when this sensitive woman rose and walked toward the young girl, the apparition didn't move away.

She asked the young child, "Why are you here?"

"I'm afraid of going to hell," the spirit allegedly replied.

There was an awkward silence for a period of time.

Then, with the girl's spirit hovering near, the group began to meditate and, in the librarian's words, cast a "white light of love" upon the girl, wishing her to find peace.

The figure vanished.

A short time later, some tenants who were residing in the former schoolmaster's home, now an apartment, came into the library and entered into conversation with the librarian there. The conversation moved about, but soon settled on an experience the residents had one evening before. Coming home along Church Road, they were startled to see a young girl standing by the union cemetery wall and looking afraid. After some moments, the child vanished.

Asked what the apparition looked like, they described to the librarian a young girl dressed in clothes identical to the entity that had appeared in the library kitchen!

Another tale has been told from the building that leaves one chilled and wondering what happened to the individual whose spirit embarked on a present day, ghostly haunt that terrified one unlucky borough office worker.

It was late in the fall after the sun had set and darkness descended upon this small community. A former borough office worker sat at his desk busily trying to finish some paperwork before heading home for the night.

From the confines of his office, he heard the usual sounds of the footsteps of tenants walking in the apartment above interspersed with the rattling of pipes as the heat in the building turned on and off.

Then, distinctly, he heard an unusual sound coming from the vacant library on the second floor. Surely it was the sound of furniture moving— perhaps even footsteps or something else… clear and intriguing yet out of the ordinary, but a sound unable to be truly described.

Now curious, he rose from his desk and entered the large downstairs meeting area, listening intently. The noise persisted.

Slowly, he crossed into the main hallway and began climbing the creaky staircase to the heavy double library doors above. Once there, he leaned against them and listened.

There again, the footsteps could be heard. With his heart pounding, he grasped the knob of the door in his sweating hand and pulled the heavy entryway open.

His eyes settled and peered into the darkness of the room, pierced only by the soft glow of an exit sign and the security lighting.

"Hello," he called out into the cavernous space.

Silence.

Again he said, "Hello?"

No one answered and the room was still.

Even slower now, he stepped inside and moved to the right of the room toward a cluster of furniture where visitors could sit and peruse the books they considered reading.

He stopped.

Again he heard nothing.

In fact, there were no noises, no smells, and no movement of any kind.

The seconds seemed eternal as he waited there in the darkness with his senses heightened.

Suddenly he was overcome by the creepy feeling that someone else was there. The feeling was strong and wrapped itself around him as if he was covered in a cold blanket.

Hair stood up on the back of his neck. His breathing quickened. Something was there beside him, behind him.

As our human survival instinct does, his kicked in and, very quickly, he turned and ran out of the room, pushing tightly closed the heavy doors and returning to his office below.

No one had been seen entering or leaving the library.

He has not returned to the library since that night.

In 2001, the old schoolmaster's home, now the borough's apartment space, became vacant. Yet several individuals claim to have heard lifelike noises emanating from its rooms during the period of time in which the place was unoccupied by a human presence. Distinct sounds like chains rattling, faucets turning on, and hearing the toilet flush were regular occurrences. Some of those noises persist throughout the building even to this day.

Recently though, a tale has emerged from the academy building which strengthens my growing belief that the realm of the spirit world is closer than we think, and separated from us by only a simple, permeable veil—one that can be crossed.

Mark Nesbitt, author of the best-selling *Ghosts of Gettysburg* trilogy, tells the story in one of his books about a pair of Civil War re-enactors who were sitting on the battlefield on Little Round Top one evening, reflecting on the day that had passed. From the mists halfway down the hill, a soldier emerged and walked toward them. He was dressed in an almost authentic looking uniform and handed one of the re-enactors a pair of shell casings which contained actual mini-balls used as ammunition during the battle. Re-enactors carried no such ammunition. When they realized what had happened and looked back after the soldier to seek explanation, they discovered he had vanished.

Similarly, one day a borough office worker sat in the large meeting space on the first floor of the academy building sharing conversation with a good friend. They sat on two folding metal chairs in an almost empty room.

As they were talking, the light tapping sound of an object falling onto the floor interrupted the silence around them. The sound startled them and they began looking about for an explanation.

It wasn't long before they came across a black, apparently old, button.

They looked over their clothing and around the room to see if there was any way either of them had lost a button, or if there was any apparent object from which it could have fallen.

Neither of them was wearing black buttons.

No object could be found.

Could this be a button lost in the same space but at some other time in the building's past—one fallen from a child's shirt or pants, or even those of the schoolmaster?

Like photos of the past which inform our present, our experiences of the unknown give us snapshots of a different realm of being that seems to overlap, and sometimes share space in, and with, our mortal world.

Restoration Ruminations

Every town has its share of history and folklore, and sometimes the two become intertwined. History says that at one point in time, the land on which the town of Riegelsville itself rests was an alluvial deposit or, in regular vernacular, an island in the Delaware River. On that island was a Native American settlement called Pechoqueolin, dated to 1698. Local folklore recorded in the town library's records tells that this settlement and that which followed were popular with the surrounding areas as places where people would come to "have their spirits cleansed."

In 1806, the river having slowly moved its way east to its present bed, one Benjamin Riegel, a stone mason, arrived in this area and purchased land from Wendell Shank who operated a ferry across the Delaware River. The town was known as Shank's Ferry, but subsequently acquired the name of Riegel's Ferry and later, in 1916, Riegelsville.

With time, the name of the land in this area has changed. Yet I, for one, believe that though you can change a town's name, or even that of a person, it is often more difficult to change one's essence or spirit. An individual must wonder what that tradition of folklore implies when it states that people came to this area to have their spirits cleansed. In a town where the dead in the cemetery outnumber those living in their homes, the thought of spirits randomly floating about town and looking for new hosts is a little unsettling. Nonetheless, if it is true that

Fig 11. The Old Piano Shop.

there is a finite amount of energy in the universe that simply changes forms, but cannot be decreased, then it is logical to assume that a spirit cast out does not go away, but simply changes or moves to a new host. Perhaps it does so randomly... perhaps not.

One such spirit seems to have settled in the old Clark and Cooley building at the center of the borough. This structure, built in 1861 by John L. Riegel, was subdivided in 1876 and sold to Mahlon Clark (Cook 140). In its history it has been a hardware store, a state liquor store, and a piano repair shop. In the late 1990s, a local contractor restored the structure. He related some mysterious events about the period of restoration.

The contractor lived in the building while the renovations were in process. Sitting in one of the upstairs rooms on a hot summer afternoon, he was chilled by a cold, bone-numbing breeze which opened the door and seemed to fill the room while creating an eerie feeling.

In fact, eerie may be the operative word for this dwelling. In one of the other apartments, the contractor and his helper painted the walls only to find the following day that the paint had run off. Now, experienced in painting, they tried again. Finally the paint held. But after the ordeal, the carpeting needed to be cleaned. When the carpet cleaner arrived and later finished his work, he told the carpenter that he felt the house was possessed, and that he wouldn't be back.

Perhaps these experiences are caused by one of Pechoqueolin's outcast spirits. Perhaps they are related to the strange footsteps and voices one older resident used to yell about from her apartment when they loudly disturbed her. Or maybe they are tied to a more interesting, yet non-ghostly discovery.

As he was renovating in the basement of the structure, the contractor was intrigued when he came across what appeared to be a bricked up door in a back room. His curiosity was peaked and he set about tearing down the bricks.

Behind the door, he discovered a narrow and long room that contained an old metal bed, a baby carriage and a tin milk jug. It seemed also that there was a tunnel beyond the room.

Having a respect for the past and not wanting to disturb or destroy the site, the contractor simply sealed the door closed again.

Apparently there is a tale in local folklore about tunnels connecting this property with the Delaware Canal a block away. Could this room have been part of the Underground Railroad? Or might it have a more sinister or frightening explanation that connects it to the feelings experienced in the rooms above?

Perhaps some day the line between folklore and history will become more defined and this room's story will be told. Perhaps then, an explanation for the spirit will be learned also!

The Riegelsville Inn

For over a hundred and sixty years, the Riegelsville Inn has stood like a bulwark on the banks of the Delaware River. Crossing the Riegelsville-Roebling Bridge from New Jersey, it is the first structure you see in town and one of its oldest establishments.

In 1838, Benjamin Riegel bought a tract of land and built this hotel and restaurant on its present day site. A haven for travelers and hungry townsfolk alike, Riegel operated the inn for three years and then leased it to another owner. The building was subsequently sold many times, but it has continued to serve the residents of Riegelsville and out of town guests in a fashion that harkens back to the days of old, yet offers modern comfort and delicacies (Cook 8).

Sitting in its downstairs bar or dining areas, one can almost hear the walls speak of the many families that have stayed under the inn's roof, or of the young couples who have sat gazing out upon the river from the 2nd floor veranda while older folks would sit on its roadside porch and rest in the evening air.

Indeed, it is not hard to imagine the richness of the fabric of stories the Inn could weave. It has been the site of joyous occasions in people's lives and has also experienced its share of tales of woe and uncertainty. Many of its floors have absorbed the tears of the broken hearted and those with shattered dreams.

Entering the Inn is like stepping through a literal portal to the past. Those who have owned it have managed to maintain an ambience of history; keeping the internal structure very much the way it has been

118

Fig 12. The Riegelsville Inn: Site of a spirited good time!

throughout its days. Walking about inside, a person may very well feel as if they are crossing through time itself and being gifted with periodic glimpses of the spirits of those who walked in those same footsteps in another era.

The tale is told of one man who climbed the staircases of the inn to its third floor. There he was startled to see a little girl, crouched down on the floor with her arms around her knees and her chin against her chest.

He asked her, "Why are you here?"

The apparition looked back at him and told the man that she had drowned in the river. The little girl then vanished.

Before its most recent incarnation, the inn had been closed for a period of time in the late 1990s. During that period, a story came to light about the similar spirit of a young girl who would follow the housekeepers about on the second floor of the inn and tear the sheets back off the neatly and newly made beds.

Could this girl be the same one who claimed to have drowned? Perhaps since she feels unrest, she believes others should too.

One might also catch a glimpse of a similarly mischievous spirit that seems to be present in the kitchen area of the inn.

The story is told of one worker who described being in the wine cellar stocking shelves and being very focused on his work. As he set the bottles in their proper places, a strange sliding sound emanated from the kitchen upstairs. Upon returning to the first floor, he was startled to see the coffee filter of one large pot sitting as if slid into the middle of the kitchen floor. No one else was around.

Those who work there on a regular basis say that this phenomenon happens very regularly and especially during the closing shift which, incidentally, seems to be the time to visit the inn for a supernatural experience.

Workers of this graveyard shift not only have to put up with coffee filter pranks, but they also tend to be unnerved by catching sight of the apparition of a woman who walks the dining room and bar areas. They say her flowing gray skirt moves about as she travels with her hair pulled back into a bun.

But if you're one who likes to encounter the spirit world and cannot get to the inn at night, you're also in luck. This spirit has been seen in the afternoon as well, focused on its eternal walk and enjoying the comforts that the inn provides.

Perhaps she is the wife of a spirited couple. Workers and guests claim to have encountered not only the woman in gray, but also a man and the spirits of a young boy and another girl.

One worker shared with me that the haunting goes beyond just apparitions too! Every once in a while when she was at the inn alone, she would hear the spirited voices call out her name or would be startled by their knocking on the walls outside the inn's bathrooms.

This same worker slept in Room 10 of the inn one night. As she slept, she dreamed that the little boy had come into her room and emptied a cat food dish that rested on the room's floor. The vision was clear. She could see the little boy scooping the food out and piling it beside the dish. He then laughed and ran away. In the morning, she opened her eyes and looked about the room. Reality now set in and told her that her experience was not a dream. There on the floor was the pile of cat food sitting beside its empty dish!

But this wasn't the first time that this worker had experienced something strange in Room 10. On her first night staying in the inn, she had rested in this room. Getting ready for bed, she turned off the light, closed the curtains, pulled back the covers and climbed in, and then pulled up the covers and drifted off to sleep.

She was awakened some time later to find a black silhouette standing beside her bed. The image was murky, with hints of royal blue light emerging from within its inky appearance. Soon the image of an orb seemed clear. She remembers pulling the covers back over her face and closing her eyes. The next thing she knew, it was morning and, whatever it was that had visited her, it was now gone.

There is another tale told from Room 10 about a former worker of the inn who stayed there for a period of time while fighting an illness. She had a pair of slippers with little hearts on them that would light up when one would walk. Shortly after this woman's death, the little slippers began to blink without any feet in them at all!

Then, within days of this incident, a picture of Christopher Columbus that hung on a wall in the inn seemed to slam itself down against the floor. This was despite the fact that its hook was firmly anchored, and the wire that held its frame on the wall was still securely fastened on the picture's back. The portrait had been the object of much conversation among several of the employees in the inn who didn't like it because its eyes seemed to follow you around the room. Perhaps this former worker, now passed on, decided it was time to take the troublesome picture down.

This would seem like a clever way for a spirit to gain someone's attention. It is definitely less of a chilling way to do it, than the experience one gentleman had in the upstairs men's room. The ladies' room was in use so this gentleman brought his children into the men's room to use its facilities. As he stood waiting for them, something tapped him on the shoulder repeatedly. There was no one else in the room.

Then a voice broke the silence of the moment, saying, "I just don't understand why you're ignoring me."

A similar tale is told from guests of the previous owners who claimed that the bathroom faucets upstairs would turn themselves on quite regularly.

For a good time, one could do no better than stay at the historic Riegelsville Inn. This is the place to come for fine dining and a quiet ambience—not to mention a hearty share of good spirits!

The Riegelsville Fire Company

The Riegelsville Fire Company is presently housed in a building that was constructed in 1849 as a church structure for the Presbyterian congregation in town. In 1874, the building was sold to the Durham school district and it functioned as a center of learning until the 1970s. In 1929, the building was also chartered as the local fire company (Cook 18).

Firefighters are dedicated people, especially those who are volunteers. Each time they answer an alarm, they walk the fine line between life and death.

It is most tragic when a firefighter falls in the line of duty. It is tragic too when a firefighter dies a natural death and their spirit seems to want to continue to serve.

Several of the volunteers of the fire company in Riegelsville tell the eerie tale of being alone in the cavernous engine house of the building at night and hearing disembodied footsteps echoing about the room with no visible source for them in sight.

Similarly, a tale is told of hearing footsteps walking about in the bathroom of the building. Some say it is the ghost of a firefighter who died in recent years. But perhaps it is a former congregant or student from the building's other days.

Whoever this specter is, it must have loved this building because it is intent on walking some familiar path within it. Maybe it seeks to be with friends or is vigilantly ready to answer an alarm and help others, even though its own life has passed.

Fig 13. The Old Presbyterian Church and School, Now the Fire Company.

Within a stone's throw of the Fire Company is a house that also was well loved in life by its occupant and, apparently, is loved by her in death too! Stories have emerged from this dwelling of a bathroom where the faucets simply turn on and off by themselves and the toilet flushes on its own.

The tale goes that the owner loved the house so much that she wanted to be buried within sight of the building. Upon her death and according to her wishes, she was laid to rest in the Union Cemetery across the street, comfortably close to her former dwelling. Shortly after her burial, the home began having its water problems.

Does her spirit still visit the house in which it lived for years?

If recent stories are evidence of an answer, then that answer is "yes."

The apparition of a woman has been observed walking the street between the Fire Company and this beloved house.

It was late in the evening as a local resident sat looking out at Delaware Road, the Fire Company, and the Union Cemetery. The mists were rising and not many people were out on the streets.

Movement caught this resident's eye and she focused on it, seeing a woman in a long beige coat walking west along Delaware Road. There was a hint of recognition toward this person so the resident, thinking it was someone she had watched many times walk up the road and cross the street, followed the figure with her eyes as it moved along the road.

Suddenly the figure just vanished!

There was no place for it to go, and no explanation.

Could this apparition be that of the woman who loved her home so much?

Or might it be another phantom out for its evening stroll?

The Old Kohl Bakery

Just as many of the other buildings along Delaware Road in Riegelsville have seen the businesses within them change over time, so too has the old Kohl Bakery.

Benjamin Riegel sold the lot of land on which this historic building stands to his son John, in 1844 (Cook 27). John Riegel built the original structure and sold it in 1874 to Frederick Crouse, who operated an ice cream shop from within its walls. Since that time, it has functioned as a post office, a bakery, an electrical supply business, and a chiropractor's office. The owners of the bakery and the electrical supply businesses both died on the premises.

A recent owner believes that someone from the past still dwells in the Kohl building because he has experienced several strange occurrences within the structure's walls.

It all started when he began to have renovated the second and third floors of the building so that they might serve as apartments.

One morning, shortly after the renovations were underway, the owner's secretary arrived for work at their first floor office. As she walked up to the door, the knob began twitching back and forth as if someone was turning the handle from inside. She thought sure it was the owner because of his sense of humor and so she peered into the windows to see if he was there.

No one could be seen.

Fig 14. Old Town View of Delaware Road, circa 1910. (Courtesy of Ann Anderson)

Curious, she watched as the doorknob continued to turn. Her curiosity soon turned to chills however, when the owner stepped up beside her, having just come around the corner from parking his car outside of the building.

This owner, a chiropractor, also related how he and several others heard the sound of what seemed to be a large man walking on the floorboards of the empty apartment overhead. These seemed to be interspersed with the sounds of a toddler quickly shuffling across the floor.

Then on another occasion, he arrived at the building to find that the water had been running in the apartments upstairs, though no one had been in the building.

And perhaps the most curious of all the stories told is one that tests the very fabric of our feeling of security.

One morning the owner was treating a patient in a room of the first floor office space. They were the only ones in the building. As he performed the chiropractic adjustments the patient needed, both of them were startled to hear the sound of footsteps descending from the third floor of the building. They seemed to come to a stop right on the other side of the room's wall.

The patient insisted there was someone there, despite the doctor's assurances that there was no one else in the building.

Finally, he agreed to show her that no one had been present to create the sounds. Stepping out of the examining room, the doctor went around the wall and into the stairwell where the footsteps had ended.

As he expected, there was no one there.

After a period of time, the sounds and experiences ended without explanation.

The Riegel Building

John L. Riegel demolished the original frame building on this site in 1882 and erected a large stone structure that he intended would serve the borough townspeople and the canal trade. In its history, the building has housed a variety of businesses and organizations including a drug store, a general store, a dental office, a factory, and a restaurant. It was also the original site of the Riegelsville Academy while the permanent building was being constructed on Mansion Row. In 1889, a fire damaged the structure and it was rebuilt to again provide space for many of the civic and religious organizations in town (Cook 27–28).

Currently, the building houses a restaurant on the first floor and several apartment buildings on the floors above.

From these apartments, some stories have emerged about previous tenants wrangling with the unknown.

One young couple that resided in the apartments for a time was repeatedly plagued by the smell of cigarettes. Neither of them smoked and smoking was not allowed in the restaurant below.

Even more eerie, they reported seeing a shadowy figure pass their bedroom door in the hours of night.

On one particularly unsettling occasion, they returned from work to find their toothbrushes wet, lying on the sink as if just used. They had been gone all day and the apartment had been locked.

Downstairs in the restaurant, one tale is told about a pot of soup that sat on a stove in the kitchen. They say that as the workers moved about they noticed that the pot of soup, on an unlit burner, had inexplicably begun to boil!

The Riegel Building itself faces Durham Road in town. One must wonder what changes individuals have seen through its windows as time has moved along. One change is evident in a home along Durham Road that at one time was a stagecoach stop and some say even a brothel. Currently the structure functions as a residence. From this dwelling, comes one of the most chilling tales I have heard in town.

It is said (though it may just be a tall tale) that in the recent past an older woman moved into an apartment of the dwelling and set up house, only to find her nights plagued with horrible dreams about a woman hanging by a noose over her bed. The terrors continued regularly each time the woman lay down for the night. On a whim, she decided to rearrange her bedroom one day. That night, the visions stopped.

A short time later, a mutual friend came to visit this tenant and happened to know the one in the apartment next door. Visiting with that neighbor, the friend explained the problems the woman had been having in her apartment. The neighbor seemed startled, then proceeded to tell the friend that years back, a woman had rented that apartment and, distraught, had committed suicide by hanging herself in the bedroom!

A third apartment in the same building wasn't immune to the ghostly phenomena either! In this apartment lived a young family with children. The youngest child would tell his mother each morning about the "friend" who would visit with him upstairs in the home. Over a period of time, the mother grew concerned because the child had reached an age where imaginary friends just didn't seem appropriate anymore.

One afternoon, a friend visited them who had claimed some psychic ability. A little nervous, the mother confided in her friend about the child's strange behavior and the friend went upstairs to investigate. While there, she allegedly contacted the spirit of a young man who was haunting the apartment, not really wanting to leave. When the woman came downstairs and shared the name of the spirit with the young mother, the woman looked on in shock. The name of the spirit was the name of her son's imaginary friend!

The Union Cemetery

Growing up, we often played the child's game Ghosts in the Graveyard and walked about the old cemeteries in town. Sometimes we did both together. There was nothing more intriguing and more eerie, than running about the old moss covered tombstones or going up to the windows of mausoleum doors and peering inside, hoping to catch a glimpse of bones or something equally as frightening.

There's something about a cemetery that either draws children to explore it or creates such fear in them that they never want to be near one again.

I'm not sure what the outcome of the experience was on the children involved in the following graveyard story, but it surely fell into one of these two categories. It happened in the Union Cemetery in Riegelsville and is one of several ghostly tales told from within its walls.

The cemetery was formed by the Lutheran and Reformed congregations in town in the late 1800s. Buried within its green fields are many of the historically significant individuals of the town's history.

One day in the early nineteen-eighties, either in mid-morning or late afternoon, a group of children were playing along the north to south path in the graveyard when they were startled to come upon two little boys dressed in overalls and seated on a bale of hay along the path. The boys said nothing but seemed pleasant. Nonetheless, the children were startled by their presence and ran back to tell their teachers what had

Fig 15. The Union Cemetery.

happened. The teachers then followed the children into the graveyard and to the spot where the two little boys were sitting. However, now in the place of the hay bale was a pink tombstone and no sign of the children except, perhaps, their names inscribed in the pink marble— two young twins who had died within a day of their birth.

It has also been said that further down that road and outside the cemetery walls, one can hear the sound of the clip clop of horses' hooves if an attentive ear is given in the still silence. This was the case for one town person as she sat on her porch in the late evening hours. Just barely audible, the sound of horse hooves could be heard traveling toward the cemetery along Edgewood Road. The pace was a gentle clip clop easily recognizable by the person's experience with horses. The ghostly procession continued for a short time and then faded away.

Could this be the phantom sound of horses as they carried the dead to the cemetery for their burial?

There are also stories told from the east edge of the cemetery, where many folks have claimed to see a woman in white moving among the tombstones late in the evening.

One particularly chilling tale comes from October 2002!

On this night, the library was again hosting its Haunted Walking Tours. Some friends of ours had come to the tour with colleagues from work and had shared the two hours of stories with fright and delight.

The evening was misty and, at about 9:30 P.M., the couples returned to their parked car in the lot of St. John church. Our friends got in the back seat, settling in for a short ride over the mountain to their home.

Slowly, the car pulled out the west side entrance of the parking lot and turned left on Church Road, headed toward St. Peter's Lutheran Church. Just as the vehicle passed the building, the driver swerved the car to the left and stopped dead. In a moment or two he turned right and headed out of town.

Our friends were startled but, considering the mist, they thought that perhaps a cat had run out in front of the car or something like that. Nothing was said that evening, but at work on Monday the driver's wife asked my friend if she remembered that swerve in the road.

When my friend acknowledged that she did, the woman told an unsettling story.

Upon arriving home that evening, the driver had asked his wife, "Do you remember when I swerved in the road back in town?"

She replied, "Yes."

"Did you see her?" He then asked.

Amazed, she had replied, "Yes—that woman in black carrying the parasol with slits in it."

"Yes," he said.

She then narrated that as their car moved south through the mist on Church Road that night, they were startled when a woman in a long Victorian era black dress appeared out of nowhere and stepped off the curb in front of their car just alongside the Lutheran church (ironically close to where Mary Louisa Aughinbaugh is buried).

The woman looked at them as the car stopped, then turned and walked slowly across the street and down a flight of stone steps that lead to Easton Road.

Once she had passed, and without saying a word, the driver continued home both startled and a little unsettled.

My friend was curious about this experience and wondered if this was Mary Louisa.

Who knows?

Walking along the cemetery wall after dark, one can never be too sure that the lights reflected off the tombstones or the dancing mists floating in the fields, aren't something more animated... something more lively... something spirited.

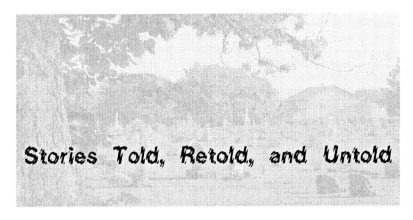

Stories Told, Retold, and Untold

Within a week of my initial experiences at the parsonage in Riegelsville, I began to journal and keep a record of all that was happening so that I could remember the stories and share them with others.

In late May or early June 2000, I had a conversation with a friend who invited me to share some stories from our house. I told a few random tales, only to be reminded by him of some others I had forgotten about but had shared on previous occasions. His eagerness over our ghost was extraordinary, considering that he hadn't personally experienced its presence here as yet.

After our conversation, I was prompted to write down a complete list of the experiences that I could compile from my journal in order to see if there were any patterns to the activity. That list turned into the outline for this book and, within a week or so, I had decided to collect and record as many stories of the supernatural as I could learn in this small town.

My eagerness to do this was increased by the fact that my wife was a member of the local library board of trustees and they were beginning to plan their first haunted walking tour of Riegelsville for October 2000. I could think of no better way to get into the spirit of such an event than to share the stories I had been telling of my own experiences over the years.

Convinced that I needed to write, I turned on my computer and began to create this book. Now some may call it being paranoid, but I had decided to save the story on both floppy disk and the hard drive of the computer just in case something should happen to create a need to recover the document. Fortunately, that's what I did.

After saving the first chapter of this book to both hard drive and floppy disk, I tried to reopen the file from the floppy disk and work further, only to find a message saying my disk drive was inoperable. It had worked perfectly for three years, but as soon as I saved this story it ceased functioning. With few options, I was forced to buy a new floppy drive. Coincidence? You decide.

In the last weeks of working on this text before sending it to the publisher, strange experiences coincided with the times in which I worked in revising it. On one occasion, I was busily working when a door to the room above me slammed open. No one else was home and the dogs were in the room with me. Another incident happened late one evening when one of our dog's tennis balls bounced down the main staircase. Both dogs were again in the same room as me. It was almost as if the spirits knew their story was being told, and wanted me to know that they were aware.

Living with a ghost has come to be similar to living in an apartment building or in half of a double home. I've come to think of many noises as attributable to other people, and that's that. The unnerving pieces of the experience are when you see unexplainable sights, when things move on their own, or when you hear strange sounds echoing in the late hours of night. This is especially true if one is alone.

Having shared with a great many people that this book was being written, I have come to believe that some folks in town see me as the "ghost man." Inevitably, when I'm approached, I'm asked the question, "So how do you explain ghosts theologically?"

My honest answer to that question is that I'm not sure I can explain the existence of ghosts. No. I'm certain that I cannot explain the existence of ghosts.

I only know that they are real.

I often wonder about all the grandness of the universe and the things I do not understand. Perhaps all time is fluid and we continue to live over and over again in the same areas, our stories being retold and relived for those perceptive enough to see them, and untold to those who are not open to them. Perhaps heaven is a place on earth and every once in a while the doors open between these two states of being. Maybe ghosts are souls with unfinished business who cannot find their way to eternal rest due to suffering, enduring trauma, or dealing with unresolved feelings.

One explanation that I have heard and do favor is that from a Native American Christian pastor who shared his beliefs with me back in 1992. He said that his belief was that, after our death, our soul travels to a river and on the other side is God and salvation. We are beckoned to cross that river. Some go quickly, others wade, and some are afraid. Those that do not cross remain in this world, but in another state of being. Perhaps that is where ghosts originate.

Perhaps they are the energy that exists after our death.

Whatever the explanation you prefer, there are ghosts in Riegelsville. These ghosts are not shy. They do appear. Some travel from building to building and keep no regular schedule, so that I could not tell you where to find them and when. Others are stationary. But they are indeed here.

If you spend time in any of the properties that line the scenic hill overlooking old Easton Road, or in some of the buildings in the town below which lie nestled between that hill and the Delaware River, you may in fact meet Mary Louisa or George Aughinbaugh, or have a visit from Marion Riegel or Cyrus Stover. You may see a phantom cat, a revolutionary war soldier, an unexplainable shadow, or another spirit cleansed or wandering for eternity—a spirit content to roam these grounds rather than take its eternal rest.

Their stories are told, retold, and untold.

Only our experiences can shed light upon them.

Yet I cannot help but wonder that if they could but speak in ways we understand, what are the stories that they would tell?

About the Author

Jeffrey A. Wargo is currently pastor of St. John United Church of Christ in Riegelsville, where he resides in the church parsonage with his wife, their three cats, and two dogs. A graduate of Princeton Theological Seminary in New Jersey, Jeff holds a Master of Divinity degree and a specialization in Chemical Dependency Counseling. He is also a graduate of the Millersville University of Pennsylvania, holding a Bachelor of Arts degree in English Journalism and Creative Writing. A native of Pennsylvania, Jeff was born and raised in Summit Hill, in the coal regions of Carbon County. In his free time he enjoys playing guitar and reading.

Printed in the United States
57026LVS00002B/280-327